INSTANT RECALL

>>>>> Tapping
Your Hidden
Memory Power

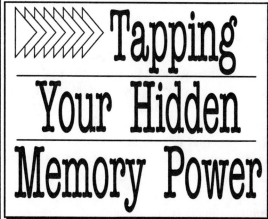

JEFF BUDWORTH

BOB ADAMS, INC.
PUBLISHERS

Published by Bob Adams, Inc.
260 Center Street, Holbrook, Massachusetts 02343

ISBN: 1-55850-010-3

Printed in the United States of America.

A   B   C   D   E   F   G   H   I   J

"It is all right for beasts to have no memories; but we poor humans must be compensated."

— William Bolitho (1891-1930)

Acknowledgments

I acknowledge the generosity of A.P. Watt Ltd., literary agents, on behalf of Crystal Hale and Jocelyn Herbert, for granting me permission to include, free of charge, in this book extracts from the late Sir A.P. Herbert's poem *The Bowline*.

I also acknowledge the kind cooperation of Mrs. Pamela Flowers, Mr. Nather George, and Mrs. Jan Grimsley, with whom I once worked, for giving me permission to tell an anecdote concerning each one of them.

Contents

Chapter 1

Your Memory: An Owner's Manual 13
Short- and Long-term Memory 14
The Dresser 15

Chapter 2

Six Guiding Principles 17
Exercise 17
Putting It Into Practice 22

Chapter 3

A Brief Tour of the Human Memory 25
Fahrenheit 451 25
Simonides and William Woodfall 26
Animals and Humankind 27
Forget-Me-Knots 29
Mighty Memory 31
The Goblin Syndrome 31
Use It or Lose It 33

Chapter 4

Association of Ideas 35
007 35
Yo-yos 36
Months of the Year 37
Heat Transfer 47
Jokes 50

Chapter 5

Mnemonics 53
Acronyms 53
Poems 55
Stalagmites and Stalactites 56
Elephants 57
Spelling 57
Words of Latin Origin 58
Hyper or Hypo? 59
Daylight Savings Time 60
Notes 61
Discarding Mnemonics 62

Chapter 6

Morse Code and All That 65
Modern Uses 65
Numbers 67
Letters 67
Phonetic Alphabet 71
Flag Signals 73

Chapter 7

Faces, Places, and Names 77
Faces and Places 79

Names 81
Learning from the Pros 88

Chapter 8

The "t-for-1" Code 91
Encoding Numbers 94
Prose 97
Keywords 99
A Party Trick 106

Chapter 9

Playing Cards 109
Number (or Spot) Cards—Keywords 110
Deck Sequence 113

Chapter 10

Exams 117
Make It Easy 118
The "Aha!" Factor 119
Use Your Five Senses 119
Choosing Books 121
Using Books 123
Rote Learning—Right or Wrong? 124
Homework 126
Must Knows, Should Knows,
    Could Knows 128

Epilogue

Review of the Six Guiding Principles 131

CHAPTER ONE

Your Memory: An Owner's Manual

"The human memory can be compared to a complex and capacious but untidy filing cabinet."

— Cyrus Lawrence Day

Beginning

Your memory, which you may consider poor, is really extraordinary. At the moment, you just don't have full control of it. As a result, it works haphazardly, but you can correct this hit-or-miss effect.

I assume you can recall scenes from your childhood; you know numerous song lyrics more or less word perfect; you can enjoy a good story, book, or film. Your memory is therefore in good working order. When you forget (or, more likely, fail to memorize in the first place) the name of a person to whom you have recently been introduced, or where you put things, that is simply because you do not file the facts away properly in your mind. If study is tedious and a waste of time, with little or nothing "sinking in," then you are merely approaching your task the wrong way.

A good memory is *not* a gift. It is a reward. Use it the right way and it will repay you.

Short- and Long-term Memory

Learn at once the difference between short-term memory and long-term memory. Your short-term memory is remarkable; it stores what I say to you, so that when I finally come to the end of a longish sentence (like this one), it makes sense because you can still remember the beginning. You may not have realized that such a process was necessary, but it is . . . and you use it subconsciously all the time.

When a school teacher challenges an inattentive pupil with "You there! What did I say?" the intended victim often turns the tables by repeating word-for-word what has gone before, even though in fact he *wasn't* listening. His short-term memory, like a tape-recorded playback, comes to the rescue.

Of course, short-term memories have very limited lifespans. What that teacher should have done was waited awhile. As a lecturer I do this myself, then later in the lesson say, "By the way, so-and-so, what did I tell you *earlier* about . . . ?" By then the unheeding student has lost whatever was said. It has been erased or overlaid by later stuff, and not stored in his long-term memory.

Real remembering involves being alert to recognize information you will need again, and, somehow or other, lifting it out of your short-term memory to file it sensibly in your long-term memory. Then you can readily retrieve it hours, days, weeks, months, or even decades later—instantly. And that's what this book is mostly about.

The Dresser

Think of when you last tidied your cluttered shed or garage, an overfilled dresser, or a chaotic filing cabinet. Imagine the dresser in your bedroom so full there is no room for another item, so disorganized that you cannot find a thing. It's time for a cleanup. How do you start?

I guess we all have similar routines. First we empty everything out, dozens of bits and pieces higgledy-piggledy, and spread them around to see what we have. We assess the available storage space. Then we start to put it all away again.

Many items obviously belong in certain places. Jackets and trousers, dresses and skirts, will go on hangers in the closet. Shoes go underneath them.

Given a nest of drawers, we put small things in the shallow top drawer: handkerchiefs, makeup, ties (unless there is a tie rack), cufflinks and belts. The next drawer down takes larger lightweight garments such as blouses or shirts and underwear. The bottom drawer is usually deeper and best for chunky woolen sweaters and other bulky clothing.

Then we are left with the awkward objects. What do you do with a hair dryer? A money belt? That black hat you're keeping for a funeral? A spare pack of cards? The birthday present that must be kept concealed until the right date? We might all differ over precisely where we put each one of these, but eventually everything will be replaced neatly and tidily, accessible, with a place for everything, and everything in this or that place.

Now let's pretend it's six months later. You are downstairs on the living room sofa, immobilized with a broken leg in a huge cast. A friend stops by and suggests a game of cards. You say, "Up in my bedroom, in the dresser, on the left hand side of the third drawer down, at the back under a blue woolly cardigan, you'll find a new pack."

Wait a minute! How do you know after six months where you put those cards? Obviously, what you actually did when you tidied up was memorize a long list of personal possessions and a matching list of individual locations. Now, half a year later, you can recall it all perfectly. Isn't that incredible? Well, not really. It is a common experience. We can all do it. But it is pretty impressive, all the same. You absorbed those lists effortlessly, without written notes, imprinting them so indelibly on your mind that you can recall any portion after a long lapse of time.

So what does all this mean?

If we can identify exactly how you did that, so you can do it whenever you choose, you may never need to work hard to learn anything ever again.

16

CHAPTER TWO

Six Guiding Principles

"Mind power is a trick. And you can learn that trick."

— Harry Lorayne

Exercise

Try this exercise. Look at the twelve words listed in the box to the right (counting multiple-word items as single entries) and allow yourself just two minutes to memorize them in the order they occur.

Do not continue reading until you have tried this assignment.

GUN
ENOUGH
FACED
APOSTLES
LETTER WORD
WAY
APOLLO
UP ON ICE
RING
INNINGS
TAKE
TOES

Now without referring back to the previous page, answer all of the following if you can.

(a) Recite the list *backwards* from memory.
(b) Which was the third word up from the bottom of the list?
(c) Which word appeared after "APOSTLES"?
(d) Name the eleventh word.
(e) Which word came before "STRIKES"?
(f) Name every alternate word, starting with "ENOUGH."

That was a hard one. How did you do? Not well, I'm guessing. Turn back and read again the difficult batch of mostly senseless words I deliberately picked for you to learn. Several, such as "ENOUGH" or "FACED," could be quite hard to picture in your mind's eye. "LETTER WORD" seems to have something to do with language, but what exactly? And what on earth does "UP ON ICE" mean? The list does not tell a story; nor can the initial letters of the twelve items be made to spell a code word. As it stands, there is no rhyme or reason to it.

You'll probably agree that learning the list in a straightforward way from beginning to end was awkward enough. If you remembered eight out of twelve, congratulations. But I'll bet you were still stumped when it came to answering my six questions about the list! To do that, you would have to know the numerical order of the words to that you could skip from item to item, backwards or forwards, without hesitation. Some feat!

But wait a minute. Look at the list once more. Now that you have a little time to think about it, "RING" might remind you of a "*three*-RING circus." Similarly, there are "*nine* INNINGS" in a baseball game, and "*twelve* APOSTLES," Christ's twelve disciples. In fact, every item on the list can be associated with a different number between one and twelve. See how they can now be rearranged.

---

1. WAY: As in "*one-way* street."
2. FACED: A "*two-faced*, deceitful person."
3. RING: A "*three-ring* circus."
4. LETTER WORD: "*Four-letter* word."
5. TAKE: "*Take five* (rest for a while)."
6. GUN: "*Six-gun* (Colt .45 revolver)."
7. UP ON ICE: "*Seven-Up* (the soft drink) *on ice.*"
8. IS ENOUGH "*Eight Is Enough* (the old TV program)."
9. INNINGS "*Nine innings* (in a ballgame)."
10. TOES "*Ten toes* (on one's feet)."
11. APOLLO "*Apollo Eleven* (the moon launch)."
12. APOSTLES "*Twelve apostles.*"

Please do not think I have tricked you into making you try to learn one list, then changing the order for no good reason. That would be unfair. There is a crucial point to be made by showing you two different lists: *memory improves remarkably if you can spot a pattern and sort out whatever must be learned.*

Time and effort spent rearranging something you have to learn is not wasted. On the contrary, learning is quicker and surer when you make the effort to systematize whatever material you must master!

Now, take your time and learn this new list, which, with its numbers, makes a lot more sense. Try to recite the rewritten list from memory, items one to twelve. If you become stuck for a word, don't worry; leave it and go on to the others. If it still escapes you, look it up and then try again. When you can recall the entire list, tackle those earlier questions of mine in relation to the revised list. They make you think, but now you can deal with them.

See how your memory improves? Yet your brain is the same. It was the systematic way you applied it that did the trick.

Try some more question. What *number* in the list is "TOES"? "GUN"? "APOLLO"? "WAY"? You see? You can do it in reverse, too; number and word are linked together in your mind. Think of one and you will think of the other.

Memory improves remarkably when you devote time to making sense of what must be learned. That valuable concept underlies everything else that follows in this book.

Don't waste your time trying in vain to hammer facts into your head any old way. A good actor or actress doesn't learn lines by mindless repetition: the key is to find out the story-line and how a given character is involved in it. Thus the speeches and chat that must be delivered make sense, as the words of the other performers on stage serve as cues to prompt the right response.

The similarities between what we did sorting out that cluttered dresser and how you came to grips with the list of words are so clear-cut that I can highlight for you the features common to both tasks. They are my six guiding principles for improving your memory.

SIX GUIDING PRINCIPLES
(Codeword: M.E.M.O.R.Y.)

1. **M** — INUTES, not seconds (allow adequate time).
2. **E** — VALUATE (take careful stock).
3. **M** — AKE AN EFFORT (be actively involved).
4. **O** — RDER THE DATA (rearrange it to make sense).
5. **R** — EINFORCE (review and repeatedly use).

    CURIOSIT
6. **Y** — (become intrigued).

Allow adequate time (M-inutes, not seconds). When you embark on a bout of spring cleaning, you set aside as long as necessary. I let you take your own time learning that sorted-out second list of words.

Take careful stock (E-valuate). The indispensable first step to tidying our imaginary dresser was spreading everything out, sizing it all up and deciding how to go about putting it back, before we did anything else. Without that forethought we would not have achieved what we did. I gave you no chance to assess the first word list and the job of memorizing it was, not surprisingly, totally unmanageable.

Be actively involved (M-ake an effort). Use these principles and it is easy to become involved in the job at hand. Once you realized the word list could be sorted into a better order, you probably thought to yourself, "Oh, I see; well, that's much easier. I can memorize *that!*"

Rearrange it to make sense (O-rder the data). You put things back into the dresser in a way that made sense to you. Although I rearranged the word list, you could follow my logic, and I'd be willing to bet that after a couple of clues you could have done it yourself.

Review and repeatedly use (R-einforce). Memory is more firmly impressed by repetition. Each successive question of mine that you answered increased your grasp of the arranged list.

Become intrigued (curiosit-Y). Treat study as a puzzle or game. Turn dull and dreary material into simpler, lively stuff. Simplify anything difficult. Then you can enjoy mastering it.

Putting It into Practice

The experimental word list demonstrated how good your memory is when you allow it to work the way it likes best. The words you learned are, of course, valueless. The sooner you forget them the better. So we will not refer to, or use, them again.

My six guiding principles, on the other hand, are indispensable. That's why I contrived the code word M.E.M.O.R.Y. to help you picture them, and why I also repeated each one of the headings and enlarged a little upon them in the notes above. We will reinforce them later on in the book.

CHAPTER THREE

A Brief Tour of the Human Memory

"Without memory there is no experience."
— William Harvey

Fahrenheit 451

In his classic science fiction novel *Fahrenheit 451*, author Ray Bradbury describes a future society in which all books are burnt, to avoid influencing and unsettling the largely submissive citizenry. (The title refers to the temperature at which paper burns.) Most people in this fantastic tale accept that the restrictions are for their own good, and even inform on neighbors who dare to own and read books in secret. Dissidents can only flee. The story ends with a fascinating account of a refugee colony, formed at a safe distance from the authorities, where every adult "is a book"—that is, he or she has committed an entire written book to memory, word for word. One man is the *Book of Ecclisiastes*, another Plato's *Republic*, a third Jonathan Swift's *Gulliver's Travels*; it takes a small group to represent the complete *Essays* of Bertrand Russell. Each one of these rare individuals is duty bound to recite his tale to anyone wishing to hear it, and also to pass it on to one of the next generation.

No small memory feat. But before the written word was widespread, races of people did rely entirely upon just such storytellers and wise men to preserve and pass on their history and heritage. These professional narrators developed extraordinary memories, devising aids to remembering that we still use today. Some appear in this book.

Simonides and William Woodfall

The celebrated ancient Greek poet Simonides lived from about 556 to 468 B.C. Although he is reported to have been of unattractive appearance, he was an excellent businessman and became the first Greek poet to profit greatly from his writing and performing. Possibly the earliest—and surely the most dramatic—account of a trained memory at work involved him. About 500 B.C., shortly after he left a banquet where he had entertained the Scopades, rulers of Thessaly, the palace collapsed, burying the host, his family, and guests. Because we today have seen film newsreels of the aftermath of earthquakes, bombs, and similar disasters, we can picture the chaos. Those digging in the rubble for possible survivors did not know exactly where to look, or how many there might be. Some of the bodies they did find were disfigured beyond recognition. Simonides, using skills that had won him 56 poetical contests, summoned up a mental picture of how the seating layout had been earlier, when he was there, and, so the legend goes, was able to locate, identify, and name all the victims.

In 1789, during the reign of England's King George III, William "Memory" Woodfall (1746-1803) established a journal entitled *The Diary*, which became the first such paper able to report Parliamentary proceedings the morning after their occurrence. He would attend the debates and then, without notes and demonstrating a capacity for vivid recall, report them accurately.

Those two historical characters are obviously supreme examples of how memory can be made to serve usefully. Understand, however, that many people in those times habitually made the effort to memorize information. They relied less than we do upon the written or printed word. We are often lost without a memo pad, notebook, or personal organizer. Now, a personal organizer is an excellent product . . . but we buy them, I think, because the marketing people have told us that it is smart and essential. The truth is we probably use only a small fraction of the contents, and could do just as well if we exercised our brains a little more.

Animals and Humankind

"I have a memory like an elephant. In fact, elephants often consult me," witty and worldly dramatist, composer, and entertainer Noel Coward is quoted as saying to John Kenneth Galbraith. The notion that elephants never forget is a persistent one. This may be a traveler's tall tale, similar to reports of the Indian rope trick. Everyone has an anecdote about it. Nobody has actually witnessed the evidence firsthand.

In fact, animal behaviorists doubt that memory plays much of a part in how animals perform. Do our pets really understand every word we say? Does a returning salmon "remember" the taste of its home river from the time it migrated—as a silvery smolt, no less—to the sea? It is more likely, according to our present knowledge, that animal behavior is stimulated by the needs of the moment. They survive on innate skills and a quickness to meet challenges, rather than from recalling past events or planning for the future. What it all boils down to is that animals may simply be very, very alert to tell-tale signals that allow them to learn by trial without much error, and so behave in ways that bring prompt rewards.

Indeed, so-called "dumb animals" can be better than humankind in some circumstances, by *not* relying upon memory. Few human beings can build a house without first serving a lengthy apprenticeship. Then it takes a team including architects, planners, bricklayers, carpenters, plumbers, and electricians to complete the project. A bird or animal that has never seen another of its own kind build a nest or lair may still do a top-notch job itself when it feels the urge to do so. Creatures rely upon fixed action patterns, triggered by the right stimulus to respond at the proper time.

This saves a lot of learning, but it has its limitations. A female rabbit plucking fur from her breast and urgently making a nest when she is not pregnant is a sight you may view as comic or sad, but it is, in the end, completely inappropriate behavior.

Humankind seems to be separated from animals by memory. In developing and relying on memory, we gave up reflex action in favor of acquired learning. So far, it has enabled us to survive and evolve.

Forget-Me-Knots

One of mankind's earliest memory aids was knots, the sort tied in string and rope. Early men used knots for hunting, fishing, and hauling loads. (There is even evidence of the use of knots for first aid and rudimentary surgery!) Knots pre-date fire, the wheel, cultivation of the soil, and harnessing the wind. Our Stone Age ancestors tied knots not only for practical purposes (much of what they made was wood lashed together with flexible reeds, vines, or rawhide strips) but also in religious or magical contexts. They also used them to pass on history and culture, and as simple but effective memory aids.

Let's say you and I are tribal chiefs meeting from time to time to discuss our mutual safety and survival. Before we part we must arrange our next monthly get-together. We cannot write; anyway, there is no postal service. We live too far apart for smoke signals or beacon fires. What's more, we'll be traveling, on the move where no messenger on foot or horseback could be sure to locate us. What can we do? Well, I have a length of twine or cord tied with 30 knots; I give you an identical one. I say to you, "Take this cord and each time the sun rises untie one knot. I will do the same. When the last knots have been untied, we shall meet here again." This ancient practice was still common in some cultures in the early part of this century; it may be that tying a knot around one's finger to remember something came about in this way.

The ancient Hebrews seem to have used knotted cords or fringes to pass on (or at least to symbolize) traditions and codes of law. It is only a small step from this to the rosary of knots or beads used in the recitation by some of prayers. The three knots in the waist-tie worn by nuns and monks remind them of their vows of poverty, chastity, and obedience. They are thus bound to their vocation, tied to their celibacy. Much of the regalia and insignia worn by military and civil dignitaries today symbolically binds the wearers to their roles and reminds them of their duties.

Memory systems were certainly taught from the twelfth century, and many races kept detailed accounts of their possessions, cattle, grain harvests, census statistics, tax details, and other items by means of colored and knotted cords. These tools were superseded by the abacus, that handy counting arrangement of rods and sliding beads on a frame. (Some scholars believe the abacus may have developed from a set of knotted cords.)

Mighty Memory

Brought up to read and write and now type on a personal computer, we underestimate the power of our memories. Stop and think for a moment about how mighty your memory really is. Try to think of all you know, everything you can recollect. There is, for a start, the accumulation of all that has occurred to you, directly or indirectly, throughout your unique lifetime; then what you know from reading and hearing about other people's experiences. You will also have knowledge, valid or otherwise, about the world in general. It seems neverending as you attempt to dredge it all up. You never reach the bottom. The capacity of your memory is vast, while the speed of recall (recognition and retrieval without first scanning every fact) can be awesome.

The Goblin Syndrome

Short-term memory has a limited capacity. It may be, however, that *all* information has to pass through it on its way to long-term storage. So a methodical approach to study is essential if short-term memory is not to be temporarily overloaded and fail you—the Goblin Syndrome.

If you're like the rest of us, you have occasionally mislaid an object, been unable to find it again despite a prolonged search, and all the time insisted that you knew nothing of its whereabouts. I know I have. We deny all knowledge of the missing item, accuse everyone else of taking it, or else resign ourselves to the fact that it has somehow disappeared into thin air never to be seen again. "There's a goblin in this house," we say. "Nothing's safe. You can't leave anything lying around; it just disappears." Later, when it comes to light in some odd place we had not thought to look, we remember—to our chagrin—that we did put it there.

The Goblin Syndrome occurs from total neglect of my six guiding principles. Here is a scenario. I am trying to complete several important tasks at once. Time is against me. Suddenly the thought pops into my mind that an overdue library book has to be returned. With only a bit of my mind on it, I reach out a hand and pick up the book to put it somewhere I will see it the next time I go out in the direction of the library. At that moment the doorbell rings. "What on earth! Don't I get two minutes to myself?" I mutter. More preoccupied with how unfairly the world is treating me than what I am doing, I answer the door. It is the paper boy; he needs to be paid. I go in search of my wife's housekeeping money. Along the way, absentmindedly, I dump the book so as to have my hands free. After paying the paper boy, I go back to where I left off. The library book is forgotten, on top of the refrigerator. As far as I am now concerned, the incident with the book might just as well have never taken place. It is out of sight and out of mind. That is the Goblin Syndrome.

Look again at the six guiding principles.

1. **M** — INUTES, not seconds (I gave no time to thinking where I put that library book).
2. **E** — VALUATE (I exercised no foresight).
3. **M** — AKE AN EFFORT (I was actively involved in paying the paper boy, but I discarded the book without any consideration at all).
4. **O** — RDER THE DATA (I put the book where it made no sense).
5. **R** — EINFORCE (I did not give it another thought).

   CURIOSIT
6. **Y** — (My interest was in other matters).

The Goblin Syndrome only occurs when the six guiding principles are disregarded. Knowing this, we can take steps to avoid it in the future.

Use It or Lose It

Some psychologists claim no experience is ever forgotten, that our subconscious harbors memories beyond recall that could be retrieved by experts. Memory is thought to be mainly a chemical process, although initial data collection via our five senses seems also to involve electrical activity. For everyday purposes, however, it seems that memory—like a computer programmed to erase data after a certain length of time—allows some unused knowledge to become extinct. This periodic tidying of the mental attic is not properly understood. It may be more likely to occur with recently acquired facts. When we study for a test, then pour it all out on exam day into written answers on paper, a few weeks or months later we have forgotten much of it. Fair enough. We may not have used or reinforced it since. What you do not use, you may lose.

Men and women with trained memories are still capable of lapses that make their friends chortle. I demonstrate memory training techniques to students in the classroom. If I take a textbook on the subject into class with me, I often leave it there by mistake. Sooner or later there is a knock on the door, followed by a gleeful, "Excuse me, sir. Here's your memory-training book. You've forgotten it again."

CHAPTER FOUR

Association of Ideas

"Ah, that reminds me . . ."

— (Trad.)

007

"I'm stuck," said one of my assistant managers. "I can't complete this form for Personnel because I don't have old what's-his-name's pay code. They have to have it today, but he's not due back from vacation for a week."

"No problem," I replied. "It's 007."

You can imagine how your reputation at work is enhanced by incidents like that. ("The guy's amazing! He know's everyone's pay code!") But that particular code stuck in my memory for a funny reason. The owner of the number had a reputation for stirring up grievances in others, but was careful never to be caught grumbling himself. You could say that he "made bullets for others to fire." So when I first heard that his pay code was

"007," it tickled my imagination. How apt, I thought. Ian Fleming's fictional character James Bond, quick-on-the-trigger (a mental association with "bullets") and licensed to kill, is also known as "007."

This association of ideas occurred to me quicker than I can write it down here (as quick as thought, literally) yet, as a consequence I can recall those figures without effort whenever his name is mentioned. Conversely, if you tell me the number I can put the right name to it. That is the useful thing about using an association of ideas. The mental link works just as well either way, as you discovered with that word list in an earlier chapter.

Yo-yos

A children's entertainer, a clown whom I meet regularly at a magic society, uses yo-yos in his act. When he heard that I collect antique ones, he asked me to bring some along for him to see.

"I'll bring them to the next meeting," I promised.

I made a mental note to do so (but wrote nothing down) and did not give it another thought until I was getting ready to go out to that meeting a month later, when the thought "I must take those yo-yos" came into my head.

How was it done? Easily. I knew I would have to go to my den to pick up one or two conjuring knick-knacks before the next meeting. I always do. So, while still speaking with him, I just pictured myself collecting that paraphernalia and some huge yo-yos at the same time. The trick is to pick and picture a place where you will certainly be at the moment you must think about the yo-yos, or whatever it is you're trying to remember.

Why not simply use a diary or write yourself a note? That would be all right if you could be sure that you would see it again at the right moment. But it is not foolproof. You might misplace it—beware the Goblin Syndrome—or put the note somewhere so "secure" that it does not see the light of day for a year. (How many times have you slipped something into a rarely used pocket of your wallet or purse, only to find your "urgent note" months later when it no longer makes any difference?)

A mental association of ideas is the best method. Concentrate on your chosen image for a few seconds. Do not let your mind wander. Then let it go. When you need it, it will come to you.

We are continually let down by people who fail to keep their promises. We become resigned to the fact that messages will not be passed on, phone calls will not be returned. How refreshing it is to deal with someone who does remember obligations unprompted! Naturally, we give them our business and our friendship. Now you know how to do it.

Months of the Year

Suppose you have, in rough order for carrying

them out, the following dozen errands to run tomorrow:

1. Take a reference book from your home to work where you need it.

2. Visit the post office to buy eight first class stamps.

3. Complete an annual leave application form and submit it to your department head.

4. Visit the optician on your lunch hour.

5. Renew your membership at the local health club.

6. Pick up some coffee and a box of doughnuts for the office coffee club (tomorrow is the first day of your week to do the shopping).

7. Make appointments to see two new employees and discuss their progress.

8. Complete annual statistics and forward them to the company's finance department.

9. Return a telephone call.

10. Look closely at the map in your glove compartment before you go home (you want to see if you can find an alternative route that avoids an awkward left turn across a busy main road).

11. Pick up the cat from the vet.

12. Reset your alarm clock for an early start the following day.

This job list cannot conveniently be arranged to make better sense, but to memorize no more than twelve items at a time, you can use another mnemonic link. (For more on mnemonics, see the next chapter.)

Which twelve nouns do we also represent by numbers—and so often that we use the words and numbers interchangeably? The months of the year! Anyone writing a date on a letter, or beside his signature on a form, has to decide whether to write the word for the month or to substitute its number.

Here, much of the "work" of memorization has already been done for you. You know that March is three, August is eight, ten is October, and so on, almost without thinking. If you settle on a distinct mental picture of each month, then, by linking these pictures with the items you want to remember, you can keep them in strict numerical order. (And, of course, recall any item by its number on the list!)

1. JANUARY	7. JULY
2. FEBRUARY	8. AUGUST
3. MARCH	9. SEPTEMBER
4. APRIL	10. OCTOBER
5. MAY	11. NOVEMBER
6. JUNE	12. DECEMBER

I have a clear mental image for each month. I will tell you what they are, but they are personal and may be of no use to you. *You must make the images your own!* Mine are:

1. *JANUARY* is the start of the New Year, so I picture Times Square—more specifically, the huge crowd massed beneath the ball that drops at the stroke of midnight on New Year's Eve. (Often, I will replace the ball with the item to be remembered—or see myself standing in a crowd composed entirely of the items to be remembered, waiting for the ball to drop.)

2. *FEBRUARY* is the shortest month of the year, with only 28 days (29 in leap year). I think of the Munchkins from *The Wizard of Oz*; I link them to the second item on my list.

3. *MARCH* is easy. I imagine a loud marching band marching down the main street of my town. (Often I will simplify this by picturing a large trombone on the main street in combination with item number three.)

4. *APRIL* is often a rainy month. For number four on the list I drench the sidewalk outside my office with April showers, and link that picture to the item.

5. *MAY* brings to mind the rhyme, "April showers bring May flowers." I set the fifth object among such flowers, in my garden.

6. *JUNE* is a woman's name, of course, but I don't happen to know anyone named June. It does sound something like the word "chewin' "; I picture myself chewing whatever the sixth item is. (The picture should be illogical, so if the sixth item happens to be any type of food, I make the item huge—the size of a small motor home—and chew on that.)

7. *JULY* is the month we celebrate Independence Day. I link our local fireworks celebration to the seventh item on the list.

8. *AUGUST* is the month I usually take my vacation. I usually go to Hawaii, so I picture item number eight in conjunction with a certain volcano I usually visit at least once during my stay.

9. *SEPTEMBER* is the month children go back to school. I link the ninth item on the list to a particular classroom and teacher of mine.

10. *OCTOBER* is Halloween. I link the tenth item to the idea of trick-or-treaters coming to my front door.

11. *NOVEMBER* is the month we celebrate Thanksgiving. I picture my family gathered around a well-provided table and link that to item number eleven.

12. *DECEMBER* is Christmastime. I picture

myself in front of the tree, opening gifts, one of them is the twelfth item.

Here is how I would memorize, in just a few minutes, using no notes, that day's list of errands I gave earlier.

1. I am standing in the cold of Times Square on New Year's Eve with a huge crowd. We look up at midnight, but instead of the bright red ball that usually descends, we see a huge neon reference book dropping down to mark the new year.

2. I am standing with Toto in my arms in Munchkinland. The Mayor of Munchkin City brings me a stamp the size of a *Life* magazine and asks me to lick it for him. I do, and it tastes horrible. I think to myself how sorry I would be if I ate ("eight") the huge stamp! (Absurd, isn't it? But it works.)

   (Incidentally, I ask myself "What is number two on today's list?" just as soon as I have recalled and carried out number one—that reference book—so as not to miss any deadline.)

3. I am at my desk trying to fill out a leave application form, but instead of a pen I am using a shiny new trombone.

4. I leave my office and am greeted by torrential rain; it streams down my spectacles, blurring my vision and flooding my eyes

with water. I cannot see; I have to go to the optician.

5. There is a bank of flowers—no, better yet, a swimming pool full of giant flowers in my garden; I must plunge head first into the pool to swim crawl stroke. That reminds me that I must renew my health club membership.

6. I am in the supermarket trying to chew open a can of coffee— without much luck. In disgust, I throw the can of coffee through a huge doughnut, much to the puzzlement of my fellow shoppers. Everyone is staring at me; all I know is that I must get coffee and doughnuts.

7. The two new employees have not worked out well; accordingly, I take them to the open field where we hold our fireworks displays every year, tie them to large sticks, attach fuses at the base of their jackets, and ignite them. They soar into the sky and explode in an extravaganza of color. (There is a certain amount of discreet wish fulfillment involved with such links, but that often helps!)

8. Standing with my wife in front of that volcano in Hawaii, we notice rumblings beneath our feet. A quick check of the top of the volcano confirms that it is erupting . . . but instead of lava, huge calculators are streaming down the sides! I pick up one of

the steaming calculators from a flow in front of me. Time to complete the annual statistical report!

9. Sitting at my desk in my fifth grade elementary class, I am surprised to hear a phone ring from within the desk! The class activity stops dead; I have to open the desk and answer the call. That reminds me, I need to return a call of my own.

10. A trick-or-treater comes to my front door dressed as a street map. Check that; he *is* a street map. I pick him up and fold him into a small rectangle, then go out and place him in the glove compartment of my car. I must look up that alternate route on the map.

11. Everyone is seated around the Thanksgiving table, and the big moment has come: it is time to remove the silver cover from the dish holding the turkey. But what's this? The cat is sitting on the serving dish, mewing loudly at the sight of that long knife! Of course, the cat has somehow wandered back from the vet.

12. The children are pestering me to let them open their Christmas presents. Which one will I hand them first? That's easy—the one that's just started ringing insistently. But first I have to find it! Once I do, I hand it over to my youngest, who is perplexed to have received an alarm clock.

Using the months of the year as a mnemonic, you can either commit all twelve tasks to memory at one time, or store them away as the need arises.

A word is in order on the links I used above. My guess is that, simply because you read over the material attentively, you are now quite comfortable rattling off items from the list at random. (What was number four? Well, four is April; April showers; rain in eyes; glasses; optician. I hope you're proud of yourself!) The reason they come back to you quickly is that each link is a strong and memorable image. Below are some keys to composing good pictures of your own. (After all, the point is not to use my images, but ones that mean something to you.) You can use the acronym C.R.I.S.P. to help you recall the various points necessary to form a fresh, *crisp* mental picture. Try to incorporate as many as possible of the following:

> C — onflict or violence.
>
> R — eaction.
>
> I — mplausibility.
>
> S — enses.
>
> P — lace.

C — *onflict or violence.* There's no need to get gory unless you feel it helps you, but notice that simply seeing a trick-or-treater dressed up as a map is nowhere near as memorable as actually folding such a person in half, and half again, and half again, until he fits in the glove compartment!

R —*eaction.* Most of us can recall frightening or embarrassing moments much more clearly than run-of-the-mill events. I was embarrassed at the stares of my fellow shoppers in item number 6; I was frightened at the prospect of being punished for disrupting class in item number 9.

I —*mplausibility.* Every single one of the images is wildly implausible. I did not attempt to picture myself simply sipping a cup of coffee at my breakfast table. That could happen! I looked instead for something absolutely ridiculous, like gnawing on a tin can in the middle of a supermarket aisle.

S — *enses.* Whenever possible, I involved sensory perceptions supplementing the visual material in the image. For instance, I tasted the foul glue on the back of the stamp.

P —*lace or object.* Each of the final images is connected to a specific physical place that I have been. For some reason this helps one retain information more readily. (Familiar objects, such as the coffeemaker on your kitchen counter, work well, too.) I wasn't just jumping into any mass of flowers, but a swimming pool filled with flowers that had somehow materialized in my garden. Making the effort to "deface" a known place in this way helps the information register clearly. Some people create literally hundreds of sequential pictures for memorization purposes by imagining various objects in their home. This can indeed be an extremely effective approach.

Unless the picture had some special meaning for you, it would *not* be a good idea to try to remember the first item on the list—the reference book—by picturing yourself holding the book and a glass of champagne (to celebrate the New Year). On its own, this image fails every single one of the tests in the C.R.I.S.P. list.

- C — *onflict or violence.* The picture is innocuous and incorporates no action at all, much less any conflict.

- R — *eaction.* There is no overriding emotion associated with the picture. (No one has even proposed a toast yet!)

- I — *mplausibility.* You could conceivably find yourself in this situation.

- S — *enses.* There is no dominant sensory element to the picture—you are only holding the champagne, but have not drunk it.

- P — *lace.* You are not situated in a place or near an object familiar to you.

Heat Transfer

In the physical world heat transfer happens in one of three different ways:

1. CONDUCTION
2. CONVECTION
3. RADIATION

Bear with me, even if you're no science student: let me show you how I remember them. These are words that any reasonably well-informed person should know. Take advantage of an easy physics lesson and learn a little more about remembering things at the same time!

1. Conduction

Hold the narrow end of a teaspoon that is immersed in a cup of your favorite hot drink. After a short time, the uncovered end you are holding between your fingers warms up; eventually, it will become unbearably hot. The heat is transferred from one end of the spoon to the other by *conduction*.

It works this way. The heat causes the metal atoms making up the bowl of the spoon to vibrate. These vibrating atoms in turn cause the atoms next to them to vibrate, and this increased motion is passed—or conducted—rapidly along the stem to you, giving the sensation of heat moving along the spoon.

I remember that this effect is conduction by picturing in my head a line of standing passengers on the packed commuter train I take every morning. More people have to get on; the conductor has to stand in the door and shout, "Move down, please!" This is very unscientific, but seeing the atoms as people on a train ordered to move by the

CONDUCTOR tells me that the effect is conduction.

2. *Convection*

Put a saucepan of water on to boil. (Ignore for now the fact that the saucepan itself will get hot by conduction.) The heated water at the bottom of the pan will rise, making way for further cold water to move in and be heated in its turn. The circulating water is moving in *convection* currents. Warm air in a room acts similarly, moving away from the source of heat and warming up the whole room in a short while.

To remember this stretches the imagination. "Convection" is a specialized word, not one that crops up in everyday conversation. No mental picture comes to mind immediately. The closest word I can think of is "confection"; cotton candy comes in the cloudlike shape I can associate with water or air convection currents. My chain of thought goes:

Currents of gas/water . . . like huge clouds of cotton candy . . . confection . . . convection currents.

3. *Radiation*

The transfer of heat from a hot to a colder body when they are not in contact (for example, the earth warmed by the sun, or, on a much smaller scale, toast under a red-hot grill) is done by *radiation*.

This is easy to remember. Radiation occurs in space even though it contains no air. Heat radiation is, in fact, similar in character to radio or television waves or light waves. Waves are emitted by the hot

49

body and transmitted through space, undetected until they fall on another body.

We know a lot these days about harmful radiation (like nuclear fallout) as well as the safer kinds (for instance, sun tanning in moderation). I just recall that my hour or so on the beach is a sort of radiation, and picture myself wearing heavy fallout gear while reclining near the shore.

Jokes

The association of ideas is a good way to remember jokes. If you are one of those who say they have heard hundreds of jokes but can never think of one to tell, try filing jokes away in your mind in categories such as "dog jokes," "airplane jokes," "jokes about spouses," and so on. Then, when a conversation drifts around to the subject of dogs, you can say, "You know, you mention dogs; I heard about this dog . . ."

Finally, on the subject of telling jokes, there is the story I first heard at school over 40 years ago. It has to do with a newcomer in prison who hears the lifers taking turns over dinner calling out different numbers. After each one there is a gale of laughter from the other inmates.

He turns to the fellow next to him and asks what's going on. "We're telling funny stories," his companion replies. "Only we know one another's jokes by heart after all this time together, so we've numbered them, and now we just call out the numbers."

The new arrival decides to give it a try, so he calls out a number. It is met with silence. He tries another. Still no sign of amusement.

"Why do they laugh at the others and not at me?" he demands.

"Well," says his companion, "the problem is the way you tell it."

CHAPTER FIVE

Mnemonics

"I've a grand memory for forgetting, David .. "
— Robert Louis Stevenson

Mnemonics (pronounced "ni-MON-ics") are devices such as rhymes, acronyms (code words), or other letter and word arrangements to assist remembering.

Acronyms

I work in law enforcement, and was once paid to lecture on the subject of surveillance. The word S.U.R.V.E.I.L.L.A.N.C.E. turned out, with some contrivance on my part, to have a letter for every topic I planned to discuss. I wrote these topics on cue cards to prompt me during my talk.

```
S — hadowing suspects in the street
U — ndercover observations on premises
R — eport writing
V — isits, official
E — vidence gathering
I — nformants
L — egalization
L — egal powers
A — ction to initiate prosecutions
N — ote taking
C — ourt appearances
E — ntrapment
```

I also typed up the twelve headings (as above) in the form of a handout for my students to keep as their reminder of the lesson.

Even "naughty" words can serve as acronyms, as long as they remain in your mind or are not written down or otherwise broadcast so that they might offend others. There is one four-letter word that spells out the ingredients of a criminal offense, and another that lists the British naval hero Admiral Horatio Nelson's famous sea victories in the order he achieved them. The more bizarre the mental association, the more indelible the imprint.

Acronyms are always better when their letters spell words, such as:

AIDS (acquired immune deficiency syndrome)

LASER (light amplification by simulated emission of radiation)

NOW (National Organization for Women)

Best of all are those spelling words that are relevant:

GASP (Group Against Smoking Pollution)

MADD (Mothers Against Drunk Driving)

SOS (Save Our Shores, Inc.)

Poems

One of the most familiar rhyming mnemonics must be the one by which we recall the number of days in each month.

Thirty days has September,
April,
June,
and November
All the rest have thirty-one
(excepting February alone,
which has but twenty-eight days clear
. . . and twenty-nine in each leap year).

We may instinctively know whether a month has 30 or 31 days in it, but I can still be unsure for a moment sometimes, until I run this rhyme through my head.

In the late Sir Alan P. Herbert's clever poem "The Bowline," which I recite publicly from time to time, there is a section that used to throw me. Since the poem is just thirty-six lines long, and eight lines gave me trouble, it was something I had to sort out. Here is the part I'm talking about:

> *"What ancient hairy tar, how many centuries ago,*
> *Was author of the artifice we do not seem to know.*
> *Maybe old Captain Noah, scarce aware what he was at,*
> *Thus made a grass-rope ready when he sighted Ararat;*
> *Maybe 'twas wise Ulysses when he made the sailors fast*
> *Against the songs of Sirens with a bowline to the mast;*
> *Maybe by Captain Jason was the first example tied,*
> *That some industrious Argonaut might pain the Argo's side . . ."*

I used to mix up those references to Noah and Ulysses and Jason, quoting them out of sequence so that the tale did not run true. Then I noticed the initial letters of each name: N.U.J. All that was needed, I decided, was a slight NUJ ("nudge") of a boat to snap a bowline in two. That little hint was the nudge I needed. Problem solved.

Stalagmites and Stalactites

These are the brittle fingers, like giant icicles, found in ancient caves. Created by limestone-rich water dripping in one spot, one kind projects upwards from the floor of the cave, while the other hangs down from the cavern ceiling. But which is which? And how is each one spelled?

STALA**GM**ITE
(G–round; starts as a M–ound)

STALA**CT**ITE
(C–eiling; it's on T–op.)

Elephants

The next time you go to a zoo, take a good look at the elephants. There are two kinds, Indian and African. At first glance they may seem identical, but they do have many distinguishing features: the tips of their trunks, the bulge of their foreheads, the way their spines curve. A keeper will tell you. The most obvious sign, for even the least observant person (like me), is their ears.

L**I**T T L E
(I–ndian)

L**A**R G E
(A–frican)

Spelling

You might be defeated when it comes to spelling an unfamiliar work when you know of no rule that will help you. Often, all you need is something to fix the correct spelling in your mind.

STATIONERY: has an "e" in the next-to-last syllable, as in a sheEt of writing paper.

STATIONARY: has an "a" in the same position, as in stAnding still.

PRINCIPLE: A principle is something worth PLEading for, a fundamental truth or doctrine.

PRINCIPAL: The head of the school should always be your PAL.

DESERT: means (as a verb) to abandon, or (as a noun), a waste region with little or no rain or vegetation. A desert is where you could be deserted (abandoned); what's more, a desert has less of everything—except perhaps sand—and so it's easy to remember that it has only one "s".

DESSERT: means the fruit or sweet that is eaten at the end of a dinner meal. Most of us want more desserts than may be good for us; it's appropriate that the word has a double helping of "s's".

Words of Latin Origin

Every once in a while you can surprise even yourself by digging down deep into your memory to come up with some fact you were unaware you knew.

Let's assume, for the sake of argument, that you are watching television and hear one of the actresses say to another, "Welcome to the sorority." Let's further assume that you're unacquainted with the idea of a sorority, and have no idea what the word means. If you have any familiarity with some of the common Latin-based words in our language—or, better still, remember any Latin from school—you may be able to proceed along the following mental path:

1. Latin	2. English	3. Adjective	4. Noun
PATER	FATHER	PATERNAL	PATERNITY
MATER	MOTHER	MATERNAL	MATERNITY
FRATER	BROTHER	FRATERNAL	FRATERNITY
SOROR	SISTER	SORORAL	??????????

You may not recall ever having been taught the word to complete column four (bottom right), but the correct meaning of "sorority" is probably well within your grasp: it means sisterhood. As you can see, memory often not only provides a data base of raw facts, but also can generate processed intelligence!

Hyper or Hypo?

I once wrote an article on drowning, based on my experiences as a policeman and my knowledge of lifesaving techniques. In the article, I referred to "hypothermia," which is the abnormally low body temperature that can result from immersion in cold water or other very cold conditions. When it appeared in print, the spelling of this vital word had been changed to "hyperthermia." Now, "hyper" and "hypo," when used as word prefixes, yield completely opposite meanings, so I was irritated to see this change. Then I realized that I was uncertain who was right, the printer or me. I had to look both words up in a dictionary—and I was correct all along. But the episode finally established the difference between the two prefixes for me

HYPER means "over" or "above," as in:
>*hyperactive*—excessively or abnormally active;
>
>*hyperbole*—exaggerated or extravagant speech;
>
>*hypertension*—high blood pressure.

HYPO means "under" or "beneath," as in:
>*hypocrisy*—insincerity, falseness (*less* than the truth);
>
>*hypodermic*—beneath the skin;
>
>*hypoglycemia*—low blood sugar.

It should be obvious now that the abnormally low body temperature that started all this off must be "hypothermia."

Daylight Savings Time

Isn't it boring to hear otherwise bright people reduced to helplessness twice a year when it's time to reset the clocks? "Now which is it this time, backwards or forwards an hour?" You hear this even though one of the most common and useful mnemonics is designed to solve the problem, and requires only a moment of undivided attention.

SPRING forward (the clocks go *ahead* one hour)

FALL back (*subtract* an hour)

Notes

When we talk about memorizing things, we usually want to keep things "in our heads" without taking any notes. Somehow it seems like cheating to write something down. But it's not!

Use notes whenever convenient. Write shopping lists; compile cue cards for public speaking; keep a diary. If you work as a cashier/receptionist, make sure you have a list of fees and charges and/or hours of operation handy. If you have to keep track of a lot of household tasks, leave notes for yourself; those self-adhesive memo pads—with sheets that stick to almost any surface and then can be peeled off cleanly—are excellent.

"Don't forget to defrost the refrigerator."

"Take the garbage out."

"Cancel the newspaper service."

You can even perk yourself up with exhortations when you are downhearted: "Most of the things I worry about never actually happen."

Jotting down notes might not seem much like memory training, but it can be. The time and effort spent deciding on a few key words for cue cards to lead you through the various stages of a speech or lecture, to avoid the embarrassment of coming up dry halfway through, will often ensure that you sail through with little or no reference to the notes. You appear to be a confident, off-the-cuff speaker; your careful preparation is not obvious. Formulating your notes meant using the six guiding principles. Therefore, you remembered much more of what you did.

Discarding Mnemonics

The bricklayer working full speed to pick up a quantity incentive and the gold-medal-winning Olympic sprint swimmer have something in common. The skills they acquired with painstaking effort, a bit at a time, have been practiced and practiced until they come automatically. Too much conscious thought would inhibit their performances. How they do what they do is grooved in by a lot of repetition and the ability to know something "at the back of the mind." That basic knowledge is then dealt with at a lower level of consciousness, leaving them free to consider strategy and tactics.

"Pretty soon, we're going to have to have a code word to remember all our code words," inexperienced students sometimes say to me. No, you won't! Learn from the bricklayer and the swimmer. Use an acronym or other mnemonic to memorize something you need. Later, after repeated use, you will find you no longer need the mnemonic. It has served its purpose and can be discarded. When you have looked at a few elephants and deduced their continents of origin from the size of their ears ("little" for India and "large" for Africa—remember?) the ears alone will signal India or Africa to you. "Little " and "large" will go unused.

The driving instructors at a police training school I know of teach a system of car control that always keeps you in the right place on the road, at the right speed. It uses the following sentence:

CAN MY SAFETY BE GIVEN AWAY?

The initial letters of the words stand for the six basic elements of driving technique, as I learned it.

C — OURSE (road),
M — IRROR,
S — PEED,
B — RAKES,
G — EAR,
A — CCELERATION

Each must be considered while approaching any hazard, in the order given. At slow speeds in light traffic, of course, it is possible to recite the sentence and at the same time perform the various actions. For high performance driving, however, the words must be abandoned and replaced with practiced physical skill. Once the words have served their purpose, and neuro-muscular systems have learned the routine, reflexes must be allowed to take over.

As you can see, memory training can also be harnessed to acquire physical skills as well as mental ones.

Sometimes, it seems that experts are super-human. How can court stenographers convert what they hear and see so rapidly to the tips of their fingers? The answer is by pure stimulus and response, with all intervening steps ruthlessly eliminated. The topics of the next chapter demand just that kind of skill.

CHAPTER SIX

Morse Code and All That

"To kiss a miss is awfully simple.
To miss a kiss is simply awful.
Kisses spread disease, it's stated.
So kiss me, dear—I'm vaccinated."
— (Morse telegraphists' practice piece)

Modern Uses

You might like to learn international Morse code. If you are physically active, and likely to be afloat in a boat, rambling along a clifftop, or isolated in some other way beyond hailing distance of help, Morse code could be a lifesaver. Scouts, guides, walkers, climbers, spelunkers, boaters, and all who put themselves in potentially dangerous situations, ought to be able to attract attention and signal their condition or predicament to others. Morse code can be sent with a flashlight or even by rhythmically pulling a curtain to and fro across a lighted window. You can blow a whistle, toot a horn, or wave a flag, depending on whether you are in daylight or darkness.

"Help—leg broken."
"Boat holed. Sinking fast."
"OK; no help needed."

Of course, there has to be someone on the receiving end who can read your message. But that's all the more reason to give it a try; you could rescue someone else!

Back in the 1950's when I learned international Morse code, large numbers of telegraphists were employed in commerce, industry, shipping, and the armed forces. We were almost as commonplace as shorthand typists. Fast and accurate international communications depended on all those beep-beeps.

Nowadays the code of dots and dashes devised in 1838 by painter and inventor Samuel Finley Breese Morse is not used so much. Technological advances have made it possible for the President to chat with astronauts in space as if by telephone. The piercing staccato Morse notes are no longer necessary to overcome the signal distortions that often made voice communication incomprehensible in the old days. In a way, that's a pity; knowing Morse code is still a very useful skill to have in reserve.

Memorizing the dots and dashes assigned to represent the letters of the alphabet, as well as the ten digits, looks like a mighty stiff undertaking. It is easier than it looks. See for yourself. First, look at

the numbers. You will quickly see the logic behind
them.

1: • — — — —		6: — • • • •
2: • • — — —		7: — — • • •
3: • • • — —		8: — — — • •
4: • • • • —		9: — — — — •
5: • • • • •		0: — — — — —

Numbers

Each international Morse symbol for a numeral has
five units, the dots and dashes being closely related
to the numbers they represent. Spend a few
minutes with a pencil and paper trying them out;
you will be convinced that you understand them
and can remember them.

Letters

I was with twenty other trade training recruits in a
barracks room one winter evening when our cor-
poral entered. He issued each of us a white card on
which were printed the Morse alphabet symbols.

"Learn those by tomorrow morning; the test is
at oh-nine-hundred," he said. Then he left us to our
task.

Was he being cruel or kind in deciding not to
supply any hint as to how it might be done? I still
don't know. I do know that we were up late that
night, working either in groups or alone according
to preference It was my first lesson, although I did

not recognize it at the time, in making the six guiding principles work.

What my buddies and I soon discovered was that some of the symbols are similar to others, or exact opposites, and that a few have an odd sound or rhythm that makes them easier to remember. We learned them accordingly in short order, and you can too. See the grouped symbols below.

E: •	T: —
I: • •	M: — —
S: • • •	O: — — —
H: • • • •	

(Note: S.O.S. was chosen as the international distress call because of the clear and unmistakable difference between three dots for "S" and three dashes for "O"—not, as legend has it, because it stands for "Save Our Souls." Omit the double "s" when sending it repeatedly. Just send • • • / — — — / • • • / — — — / • • • etcetera.)

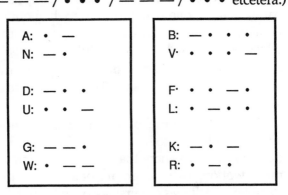

A: • —		B: — • • •
N: — •		V· • • • —
D: — • •		F· • • — •
U: • • —		L: • — • •
G: — — •		K: — • —
W: • — —		R: • — •

Some people connect the rhythm of "F" with the sentence "Did it *hurt* you?" I picture the Morse for "K" as the front view of an old-fashioned monoplane, with a round fuselage and the wings on each side. An old slang term for an airplane was "a kite." The "V" combination is almost identical to the famous opening notes of Beethoven's Fifth (Roman numeral V) Symphony. You might remember that that brief musical passage was used throughout the film *The Longest Day*, which concerned the Allied invasion of Normandy. " 'V'-for-victory" was of course a popular Allied slogan.

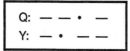

Morse "Q" sounds a little like the first four notes of the song "God Save our Gracious ('Q' for) Queen." I see "X" as an airplane's propeller and the symbol as allied to "K" (see above) but with a bigger fuselage. That leaves only three odd men out to be learned.

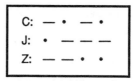

Morse telegraphists discussing the code do not say, "Dot, dash, dot." They speak it as it sounds when transmitted from a morse buzzer, pronouncing a dash as "daw" and clipping the final "t" off of a dot (pronounced "dit") when it is followed by another note. It comes off the tongue more easily that way. "L" is therefore "di-daw-di-dit"; "Z" is "daw-daw-di-dit."

Back in the barracks, having done all we could to commit our card contents to memory, we slept on it. Early the next morning we went over everything again. When we were tested, we got it more or less right, much to our relief. A few practice sessions helped us to acquire fluency, although it was to take months of daily practice of increasing speed and complexity to reach the standard needed for operational work. You do not need that proficiency. You really should try to master Morse code; you'll exercise your brain and gain a rare and valuable skill that could save a life—even your own.

It is a convention widely observed by telegraphists that you should (a) never send faster than you can receive, and (b) never send faster than the person sending to you. The verse at the beginning of this chapter was deliberately composed as a hard test for even practiced Morse operators. It uses a lot of the trickier letters (for instance, "E", "I", and "S") encoded as dots. Dots are transmitted much faster than dashes (you just can't rush "T", "M", or "O", or the numerals "8", "9", and "0"). So go easy with words like "this," "whistle," and others like them. Give the receiver's mind time to register, decode, and write them down.

A:	• —	S:	• • •
B:	— • • •	T:	—
C:	— • — •	U:	• • —
D:	— • •	V:	• • • —
E:	•	W:	• — —
F:	• • — •	X:	— • • —
G:	— — •	Y:	— • — —
H:	• • • •	Z:	— — • •
I:	• •	1:	• — — — —
J:	• — — —	2:	• • — — —
K:	— • —	3:	• • • — —
L:	• — • •	4:	• • • • —
M:	— —	5:	• • • • •
N:	— •	6:	— • • • •
O:	— — —	7:	— — • • •
P:	• — — •	8:	— — — • •
Q:	— — • —	9:	— — — — •
R:	• — •	0:	— — — — —

Phonetic Alphabet

While you're at it, take a swing at the international phonetic alphabet, too. We all occasionally have to spell out a word to someone. Use the system adopted by the professionals and emergency services, police, fire brigades, ambulance crews, lifeguards, airline pilots, seamen, soldiers, journalists, and so on. Why settle for anything less?

A – LPHA	N – OVEMBER
B – RAVO	O – SCAR
C – HARLIE	P – APA
D – ELTA	Q – UEBEC
E – CHO	R – OMEO
F – OXTROT	S – IERRA
G – OLF	T – ANGO
H – OTEL	U – NIFORM
I – NDIA	V – ICTOR
J – ULIET	W – HISKEY
K – ILO	X – RAY
L – IMA	Y – ANKEE
M – IKE	Z – ULU

To spell the name Smith over a crackly telephone line, say, "S - Sierra, M- Mike, I - India, T - Tango, H - Hotel." Nobody can possibly mishear that.

There is no shortcut for learning the phonetic alphabet, unless it is to use four or five of the words until they become second nature, and then move on to the next batch. Hearing others speak them helps; you might also choose to pick out groups of words that go together.

NAMES: Charlie, Juliet, Mike, Oscar, Romeo, Victor.

PEOPLE: Papa, Yankee, Zulu.

GEOGRAPHICAL LOCATIONS: India, Lima, Quebec, Sierra.

DANCES: Foxtrot, Tango.

GREEK LETTERS: Alpha, Delta.

MISCELLANEOUS: Bravo, Echo, Golf, Hotel, Kilo, November, Uniform, Whiskey, X-ray.

Flag Signals

While we're on the subject of signaling, we should address the code of signal flags. A working knowledge of this can be especially useful if you are an amateur or professional sailor or waterman.

Start with the alphabet. The 26 flag patterns and colors are as distinctly different as they can be—but that makes them easier to learn. Pick out similar pairs or opposites. By reviewing the accompanying chart, you'll see, for instance, that "A" and "B" have identical silhouettes, and that "P" and "S" are positive and negative images of one another. Similar shape, design, or color links exist for the pairs "R"-"X"; "K"-"H"; and "C"-"W". Take a look.

A flag's color, in combination with its meaning as a symbol, can be memorable. "B" is red. It stands for "I am taking in or discharging dangerous goods." So, red stands for danger, perhaps explosives: "B" for BANG.

"A" is blue and white. It means "I have a diver down." I imagine blue water and white bubbles from the diver.

There are many more relevant associations that can be used to memorize the flags and link them with their meanings: invent some yourself.

(By the way, if you trace the outlines of the flags, and then color them in yourself, you'll be well on the way to learning them. You need a nautical almanac to find out what signals can be made with them.)

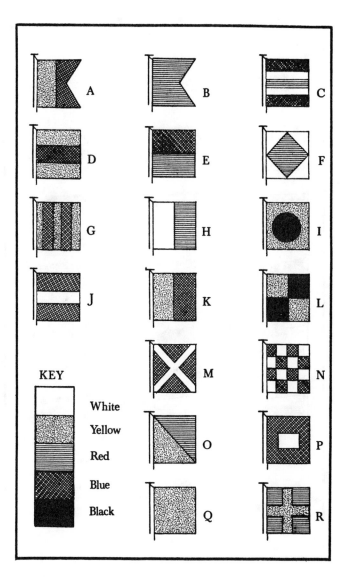

KEY

White
Yellow
Red
Blue
Black

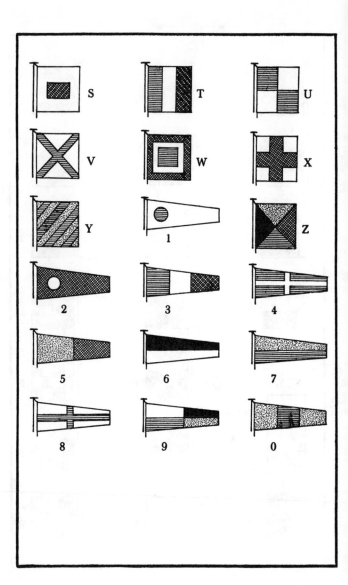

CHAPTER SEVEN

Faces, Places, and Names

*"There are three things I always forget.
Names, faces, and—the third I can't remember."*

— Attributed to Italo Svevo (1861-1928)

One of my assistant managers, when she was new to our organization and had to deal with a member of the staff she had not met, would say to me, "What's he like? Give me one of your summaries."

She had picked up on my way of seizing on a few outstanding characteristics and then sketching people's outlines in words by which a stranger could identify them in an instant. Until she pointed it out to me, I had no idea I was doing this. I guess I picked up the habit in my early work as a street cop, when the ability to radio in a quick, telling description of a suspect (". . . very hairy wrists, a far-away look in his eyes, and sniffs a lot") was a lot more helpful than talking about age, height, and build. "Medium build, about six feet tall, brown hair . . ." That fits millions of people! Tell me someone has six fingers on one hand and I guarantee you I'll be interested.

If you want to recognize a person again after a long time and maybe in another locality, when you have met him only once before, you have to play a little game. Size him up mercilessly. Pick up on the unique aspects of his appearance; ignore ordinary features. Become a mental cartoonist. Strip your subject—secretly, of course—of all dignity. "Round shoulders, bad breath, and a wart on the back of his neck with hair growing out of it."

If a person's outstanding traits are that he always radiates charm and kindliness, looks angelic, and smells alluring, then say so. Most of us, though, have quite a few flaws for the sharp observer to take advantage of. Me? Well, I'm fiftyish, but often look far older, bald, and have small ears. I talk a lot, and I wave my hands in the air when I do. My nose is like a lump of putty and I peer out over a pair of unfashionably old glasses.

Remember: we need to recognize faces a) within a short time—later at the same party, business seminar, or other outing; and b) after a substantial lapse of time, often in a totally different place. Two approaches are possible.

1. The same day, you might be able to take notice of an elaborate hairdo, a tan, heavy makeup, signs of illness, ungainly weight distribution, or skinniness. These aren't

going to change over the course of a few hours.

2. Over any length of time, though, such signs could disappear. A beard can be shaved off overnight; a certain color or fashion preference can change. To remember anyone over the long term, we have to select features that are unlikely to change greatly. The shape of a person's nose, eyes, ears, mouth, chin, cheeks, or hands will stay more or less the same from one year to the next. Adult height will be the same—except for a slight decrease with aging. Date and place of birth never change, although a liar might tell you something different. (Bear in mind that apparent age is often a better guide than actual age. A 65-year-old with crowned teeth, a jogging suit, and a good tan can look 50. A schoolgirl may appear to be 21 or even older, if she's dressed for the part.)

Faces and Places

As a rule, you will want to link face and build with where you met the person. Just about everyone has had the experience of being approached on the street by "someone we've never seen before in our lives" who nevertheless walks up, smiles, and says, "Hey, how are you doing? I didn't think I'd run into you around here!" A tricky couple of minutes of small talk follows while you pretend to recognize the person and try to maneuver him into revealing in what context you met. So: how can you link appearance with the place where you committed it to memory?

Recently, a salesman visited my office. He was dressed sharp, in a neatly-tailored sport coat, pressed slacks, a clean shirt, and a formal tie. Now forget all that. If I run into him again outside of work, he might be informally dressed. He had tightly curled hair, fairly unusual, but it was not natural and might change with time. Nothing worth concentrating on so far. Then when he reached out to shake hands, I saw that his right thumb was missing. He acted unselfconsciously about it and mentioned when I asked (I was starting to bring the six guiding elements into play) that he had lost it in an industrial accident. Later in our conversation he told me that his hobby was photographing wildlife at night. I thought to myself that that could raise problems for a man whose manual dexterity was limited. This fixed firmly in my mind that he was a photographer.

Our meeting concerned an estimate for replacing swimming pool hall lighting. I asked what kind of lighting he used for his night photography. After only a few minutes with him, I was confident I had absorbed enough to know him again at first sight: I would immediately think of his photography and—by association—my pool hall lighting. His name was Mike; it's an easy link for me between lighting and another electrical installation of mine, the public address system, with microphones (mikes). There is no doubt about it in my

80

mind now: when I meet him again, I'll know for certain that this is Mike, the salesman who came to see me at work about lighting.

He would remember me; he's a good salesman, who probably keeps a card index with me in it. As soon as he returned to his car from our meeting, he would have jotted down what we talked about, so he could refresh his memory before we met next time. (The act of writing, of course, would have helped him absorb the facts in question more completely.) All of us like to feel special, like to be treated like old friends, even if we have a feeling there's a certain amount of contrivance involved. People warm up to you when you show an interest in them.

Names

Americans are, frankly, pathetic when it comes to remembering people's names. Most of us are better with faces. Maybe other societies are just as bad, but I have my doubts. The unspoken message seems to be, "We're a proud bunch; it's asking too much to expect us to admit that we didn't get a name the first time around. Besides, who wants to buttonhole a complete stranger and make him repeat himself?" Well, pride and shyness aside, not remembering the name of someone you just met is flat-out lazy. If you can overcome the all-too-common lack of any systematic application in this area, you will have found a sure way to make yourself stand out from the crowd.

I once employed a Middle Easterner named Natheer George. George was his last name; Natheer was his first name. Everyone but me called him George because it sounded like a first name. Anyway, they had never really found out how you said Natheer. They knew it was wrong but kept on doing it, without even asking him whether or not he liked it. Strangers overhearing them assumed George was his first name. People in other departments would call me and ask, "Do you have a George something over there?" He was good natured enough to answer to his new moniker, but he must have been annoyed that we couldn't be bothered to cope with his real first name. I used it, but that caused difficulties because others had no idea who I was talking about. What a mess!

The effort to learn a person's name is repaid many times over. People like you to use their names. They don't make any allowances for "poor memory." They assume the problem is either rudeness or lack of interest. And I think they may well be right.

I'd much rather use a name and make a mistake. At least you can be corrected and learn what the name really is! And after that, of course, there's just no excuse for messing it up.

Use the six guiding principles. Take time over a new name. Get it clear in your mind: what is being said to you? Have it spelled out. Talk about it. Use it from the outset. Tell it to others.

I confess: I sometimes mix things up when it comes to names. Two female cleaners worked for

82

me, Pam and Jan. Because I was an office worker, coming in at eight and leaving by five on most days, I saw Pam every day. I rarely saw Jan, except when she came early or I worked late. Time and again, when this happened, I addressed her as "Pam." Sometimes I knew it was wrong as the words were coming out of my mouth. More often she had to remind me. It was very embarrassing: a mindless reflex that was hard to overcome.

I finally resolved that every time I saw Jan, and just before I opened my mouth, I would think to myself "Just a nanosecond." (A nanosecond equals one thousand millionth of a second.) This phrase would not only make me pause, but the initial letters of the three words spelled the name J.A.N. It was a silly idea. It takes a minute or two to explain. But it worked, and in a flash.

There are a few rare professional memory experts who give truly amazing demonstrations of their technical powers, recalling the faces and names of perhaps a hundred or more guests at a dinner or meeting, having been introduced to each one in turn only briefly at the beginning of the evening. Others (mostly stage performers) can tell you of past events in great detail by answering questions called out by the audience. Some magicians seem to be able to recite entire books by heart; many are genuine, though a few are clever showmen. But not one of these people is as miraculous as we let ourselves believe.

Human brain potential is far beyond the timid limits most of us have settled for. One psychologist stated on a recent radio talk show that he and many of his colleagues now believed that we operate on as little as two percent of our real capabilities. Incredible!

Memorizing the names of crowds isn't on everyone's list of things to do to boost productivity, but you can do a lot better with the few individuals you do meet for the first time each week. The common cry here is, "I can remember faces, but I'm no good with names." That's no excuse. Apply the six guiding principles as shown:

1. *MINUTES, not seconds.* Take your time. Do not rush introductions. Slow them down.

2. *EVALUATE.* Think: is this a common or rare name? Ask yourself if it falls into a particular category and perhaps compose a quick mental picture. *Every* name can be made to fall into one or more of the following:

   - Can it be associated with a fictional or historical character (Sawyer, Churchill)?

   - Does it remind you of an invention or event (Whitney, Lynch)?

   - Is it a synonym for a common experience, activity, or object (Snow, Archer)?

   - Is it composed of two separate pictures you can combine easily into one (Honeycutt, Slatsky)?

- Is it an abstract concept, a verb or adjective you can apply to the person in your mind (Welch, Young)?
- Can it be made to sound like something else you can picture (Pulaski [pool-ask-key], McGillicuddy [make-calico-tea])?

3. *MAKE AN EFFORT.* Write it down. Ask if you have it right.

4. *ORDER THE DATA.* Have it spelled out. Ask for a business card. Is the name on a letterhead somewhere? Is it listed in the telephone directory?

5. *REINFORCE.* Take every opportunity to use the name. Introduce the person to others.

6. *CURIOSITY.* Ask the person about himself; discover interesting facts by running through a mild and kindly interrogation.

You might try using the name categorization techniques outlined in the EVALUATE stage above to picture your new acquaintance in some memorable way.

Miss Lynch, who has a mole on her cheek, is a ferocious Cubs fan. (You could picture her in a Cubs uniform, taking the plate at Wrigley Field, with its ivy-covered walls. The pitcher throws at her cheek, aiming for the mole; the crowd, outraged, tries to lynch the offending pitcher.)

Mr. Churchill, who has a receding chin, works at IBM. (You could see your chinless cartoon image of him hunkered behind a huge computer—yours, say, as long as it's an IBM—trying to type a program with a huge lit cigar. I'm assuming that's enough to remind you of Winston Churchill; it is for me.)

Mr. Snow, who is balding, sells insurance. (See a white toupee on his head made of snow; scoop the snow off yourself with your two hands, as in the familiar "Allstate" gesture.)

Mrs. Honeycutt, who is extremely short, collects stamps. (The reason she is short is quite clear: a massive honeybee is sawing her legs off, and making you apply long sheets of postage stamps to the wounds.)

Mr. Welch, who has an overbite, is regional director of sales. (Because of his bad judgment in welching on a bet he made with you, you have sentenced him to have his top set of teeth attached to a large sail headed off into the sunset—*sales director*—and this is what is responsible for the overbite!)

Miss Pulaski, who has prominent eyebrows, is in law school. (She is working as a lifeguard at your municipal pool. You need the key to the restroom, but you lie to her and tell her the water in the pool itself needs to use the bathroom—*pool ask key*. She hands you one of her bushy eyebrows; you know that if you don't return it, she will sue you when she passes the bar.)

Of course, the pictures outlined above are not as useful as the ones you yourself create to fit a given circumstance. (And they're only memorable if you make the effort to see them in your mind's eye vividly.) The point is that the abstractions of any name can be combined with the observations you make about people; once you can make the result memorable, you will have found the solution to the problem of forgetting who people are and in what context you were introduced.

Note that eyes are better then ears when it comes to remembering names. Eyes feed our brains with images rather than sounds. We can turn words into pictures by writing names down, taking a business card, and so on.

Ask questions! If your new acquaintance's name is Allen, don't just assume you have the right spelling. Make sure.

"Is that with an 'A' or an 'E'?"
"E."
"So: l-e-n?"
"That's right."
"Two 'L's'?"
"Yes."
"A-l-l-e-n."
"Right."

Once you have taken the trouble to establish that he is Allen and not Alan, it's smooth sailing!

My family suffers endless irritation from having its last name misspelled and misspoken, even by those who have seen it written down at some time or another. I type it on my letters, but the replies come back addressed "Dear Mr. Butterworth" (or Budsworth, or Buckworth, or Bloodworth, or Bidworth, or any of a dozen other unlikely permutations). The writers just plain don't pay attention—or maybe they think they know best. It's extremely annoying!

A few years ago I took on a stage name: Bud Worth. People have no difficulty with that, whether they see it written down or just hear it spoken. Well, now: it's the same name, only broken into two parts. As we saw with Mrs. Honeycutt in the image I gave you a little earlier, once you break difficult names down in this way, they're much easier to grasp. (By the way, what was the bee making you apply to her wounds? You now remember Mrs. Honeycutt's hobby, and can use that to break the ice with her when you next meet.)

Learning from the Pros

You're watching a film; someone knocks at our heroine's door. She opens it. The man standing in the doorway says, "Mrs. Smith? Mrs. *Jennifer* Smith?" Immediately we know that the visitor is an official representative of some sort, probably a policeman. Playwrights and directors use the device over and over again; it may seem timeworn, but as we now wrestle with the problem of pinning down names in our minds, it's a good example to follow. Professionals in the name game—police-men, social workers, reporters—are experts. We can learn from them.

New officers in my precinct were always taught to go through the following routine:

"What's your full name, please?"

"Anne-Marie Betty."

"Is Betty your last name?"

"Yes." (We had to underline or print surnames so that there was no confusion later when, as in this case, a last name might also be used as a first name.)

". . . and is Anne-Marie your only first name?"

"No. My middle name is Peggy, but I hardly ever use it."

"Is it actually Peggy, or is that a variation of Margaret?"

"No. Peggy."

"So it's Anne-Marie Peggy Betty."

"Yes."

"How do you spell Anne-Marie?"

"A-n-n-e, hyphen, M-a-r-i-e."

". . . and Peggy? Is that P-e-g-g-y?"

"Yes."

"And Betty . . . B-e-t-t-y?"

"That's right."

"Thank you, Mrs. Betty. Now, could you please give me your full street address?"

And so on. It seems like a long procedure for something so simple. But that's the whole point. Unless you concentrate on something and make a big thing of it—taking minutes, not seconds, and using all the guiding principles—it is just too easy to make mistakes with names over and over again. Make the effort as I've outlined here, and you only have to do it once.

CHAPTER EIGHT

The "t-for-1" Code

"Tell me not in mournful numbers . . ."
— H. W. Longfellow (1807-1882)

Before we get started with this chapter, I want to share something that's come to mind about Longfellow; the quote above got me thinking about him. Look at his initials. Now consider that he wrote the poem <u>Hia</u><u>W</u>atha. Wouldn't that make it easier to remember the connection between author and poem? This is a good example of the way association can occur quickly and easily.

Learning words is easy when one idea leads logically to another. It's even easier when the words rhyme, especially if they're set to music. (Now you know why the pop ditty you hate kicks around inside your head all day after you hear it on the radio in the morning—though heaven knows you never made any effort to memorize *that!*)

Prose that makes little or no sense—such as legal or technical texts and bureaucratese—has to be simplified. Numbers can be even more of a problem. If you don't work regularly with long columns of figures, or have a deep interest in math (and most of us don't), memorizing numbers can be a real pain. Fortunately, there is a way to make remembering them fast and reliable.

We are about to examine the most powerful trick I know for developing a remarkable memory. It is a system that substitutes letters of the alphabet for numerals, so you can *read numbers as words*. With it, you can quickly learn lists of numbers or objects, recall the order of playing cards, and even retain difficult chunks of written text. It is known as the "t-for-1" code, because the number one is encoded as the letter "t" (or the phonetically similar "d").

The code is thought to go back to at least the 1600s; since then it has been used by all kinds of people to great advantage, and is now taught in any number of settings. What we are about to discuss is the single most valuable tool available to anyone wishing to improve memory ability.

I came across the code by chance when I was 25, learned it in half an hour on a train ride, and was fluent enough to use it a few days later. It's actually very simple; you can grasp it as easily as I did. Here it is:

1	2	3	4	5	6	7	8	9	0
t	n	m	r	l	j	k	f	p	s
d					g	g	v	b	z
					dg	c			c
					ch	ck			
					sh	qu			

Note: the "g" used instead of six is a soft one (as in George), but the "g" and "c" used for seven are hard consonants (as in Greenland and Camelot).

You can learn the code in a few minutes once you spot a connection between each digit and the letter replacing it.

t is 1 because both are written with a single downstroke.

n is 2 because both are written with a single curve.

m is 3 because both have two distinct curves.

r is 4 If you can roll your "r's" in speech, then "r" can become the dominant letter: "fou*rrrr*."

l is 5 Latin L = 50.

j is 6 "j" can be handwritten as a mirror-image of 6.

k is 7 The first upright stroke of a capital "K" can be written like a 7.

f is 8 A longhand "f" has two closed loops, like an 8.

p is 9   "p" can be written as the reverse of a 9.

s is 0   The letter that is all curves represents the number that is all curves.

Encoding Numbers

To read a number as a word, replace each of the digits by one of the appropriate consonants shown on the table above. Then insert any vowels that will make a word. Let's take the number twelve, for example, which becomes t-something-n (or d-something- n); a lot of words are possible.

TAN	DEAN	DAN
TON	DIN	DON
DEN	TIN	

Vowels don't count, so you can add them at the beginning or end to make further words.

TINA	TUNA	ODIN
TONE	EDEN	DINE
DANE	DUNE	ATTAIN*
DONE	TUNE	

* The "tt" can still only stand for one, since the code works by sound and *not* by how the word is spelled.

The only strict rules are that you must keep the "t" (or "d") and "n" sounds in the right order (to avoid confusing 12 with 21, for instance), and you must never accidentally introduce any letter that represents another numeral. "Dance" may come to mind because it has the first two sounds in the right order, but it can only be decoded as 120.

Any one of the words in the above boxes can be read as twelve, and only as that number. Suppose you're trying to get a date from someone of the opposite sex. You overhear the address and want to be sure of remembering the house number on the street without telltale note-taking. You could use TAN if he were brown, or DANE if she were blonde, or EDEN if you pictured the two of you living happily ever after. The whole exercise boils down to mental pictures—pictures that work for *you*. You have to pick a word that springs to mind the moment you think of him or her . . . and it has to decode to twelve.

So far, I haven't mentioned a few consonants:

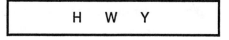

Like vowels, these can be used without affecting the numerical value of words. (The letter "X" would transcribe as seven-zero, following the pronunciation rule.) This leaves us with even more possibilities for twelve.

WOODEN	WHEATENA
HIDDEN	DANNY
TINNY	HAYDEN
WHITNEY	

Suppose you're sitting at home watching the game show *Jeopardy*. The category is the Civil War; the emcee reads from the board:

Year in which the first shot was fired on Fort Sumter.

When the contestant pipes up with the correct response ("What is 1861?"), a thought crosses your mind. The word "shot," central to the puzzle, happens to transcribe to 61! If you needed to retain that information for a test, you would have uncovered a good association.

You meet an accountant friend at a party; he tells you that he's just moved, and has a new phone number to give you. It's 459-2670. Instead of writing it down, you might think to yourself that an accountant has to *really punch keys* to get the job done. Of course, you may not always be able to make such an apt link. But with a little improvising, you could make that picture fit even if your friend was, say, an advertising executive. You could see him punching his keyring in frustration at having lost an account; you could see him working late at night in front of his computer keyboard to finish a campaign; you could even recode the number to something else that you found easier to retain:

```
4 (r) 5 (l) 9 (p/b) - 2 (n) 6 (j/sh/ch) 7 (k/g/c) 0 (s/z)

            real banjo case
            roll up no checks
            Harley up on shocks
            harelip: no cheeks
            Ray will pinch cows
            royal piano chokes
            earlobe now shakes
```

More than one theatrical mind-reading act has depended on this code. I bet I can read *your* mind at this very moment. You're thinking to yourself that this seems like a lot of trouble to go to just to memorize a few numbers. But please keep reading! The code can also help you learn prose.

Prose

To pass a test, I once had to be able to write down, from memory, the four aims of a particular industry organization. The aims of the council in question were to:

1. *Promote general understanding* of the social importance and value of sports and physical recreation;
2. *Increase the provision* of new sports facilities and stimulate fuller use of existing facilities;
3. *Encourage wider participation* in sports and physical recreation as a means of enjoying leisure;
4. *Raise standards* of performance.

The group didn't actually number its aims; I did that to make it easier to apply the code. I only memorized the parts I've italicized; these headings acted as cues for me to recall the rest. (Of course, it helped that I was familiar with the organization; if I hadn't been, I might have needed to memorize more.)

Here's what I did. The number one encodes (among other things) to the word "tea." I pictured in my mind's eye a great big glass of iced tea. To cope with the words "Promote general under-standing," I concentrated hard—for a few seconds only—on a mental image of an army *general*. He's a ridiculous little figure, barely one foot tall, *standing underneath* his horse. He is drinking that iced tea. Some V.I.P.s are *promoting* him to Field Marshal (or whatever they promote generals to). Now, if you ever ask me what the first aim of that industry group is, I'll come right back with "Number one: promote general understanding of . . ."

Do you get it? Just as with all association of ideas, you must link together two vivid mental pictures. Only now, one is a number and the other is the fact you want to recall. If you have one, you'll have the other. If you had asked me where "Promote general understanding" comes in the list order, I'd have had one thing and one thing only to say: number one. The two pictures (iced tea and the general) are inseparable, and tea can *only* mean one.

Here's how I memorized the other three aims.

Number two can be represented by the word "Noah." He took two of every species aboard the

Ark to propagate them. I formed a childish image of Noah and his Ark surrounded by multiplying creatures using sports equipment ("Increasing the provision . . .").

I use "May" (the month) for number three, picturing a garden walk I knew well in my childhood. The fragrant flowers automatically signify the month of May to me. (Mental associations have to be like that; your own are best.) "Encourage wider participation . . . " is a vague phrase to memorize; it took some imagination to link it to a May blossom. Then it came to me. That particular walk is a tourist attraction. Each year, when the blossoms are at their best, the local papers tell everyone to go and see them while the display lasts. This encourages the maximum number of people to go and enjoy the sight ("Encouraging wider participation . . .").

I read number four as "ray." I imagine the sun's rays falling on a banner being hauled up a flag mast ("Raising standards . . .").

You can astonish people with your memory if you adopt this code. But remember: a good memory is *not* a gift. It is a reward. It works when you concentrate, forming pictures in your mind.

The "t-for-1" code works best when you numbers into words that are *nouns*—nouns are easier to picture.

Keywords

When you become quick at making memorable— even outrageous—mental links, you will probably find that it's simpler to use the same word for the same number all the time. Rather than waste time trying to come up with the right word every time, settle for one word and make it fit what you want to commit to memory.

Here are my keywords up to 10 used with a sample list of items. Read the list and envision the pictures I suggest as you go along. You'll reinforce the basic sound patterns, of course, but you'll also see just how powerful keywords can be.

1. Tea (Item to be remembered: washing machine.) You are throwing dozens of full glasses of iced tea into your washing machine; you slam the door, hit a button, and listen to the loud crashing and breaking sounds that follow.

2. Noah (Item to be remembered: magazine ad.) No animals show up for Noah's cruise, so he has to take out a full-page recruitment ad in *Newsweek* (or any magazine you subscribe to; see the photo of old bearded Noah as you hold the magazine in your hands.)

3. May (Person to be remembered: chauffeur.) A huge flower is driving you to work in a limousine, attracting much attention on your arrival.

4. Ray (Item to be remembered: medicine.) The sun's rays are black; it's sick. You offer the sickly sun a spoonful of medicine,

which it swallows obediently. Sunbeams appear!

5. Leo (Person to be remembered: Marilyn Monroe.) Recall the famous subway grating scene from *The Seven Year Itch*. Only it's not Monroe standing over the grating, but a lion (I use Bert Lahr as the Cowardly Lion) trying to keep its skirts from swirling up.

6. Jaw (Person to be remembered: queen.) For some strange reason, the Queen of England walks into your place of work, locates you, and socks you right in the jaw.

7. Key (Person to be remembered: Michael Jackson.) The pop star's latest media stunt is to ask you to sew your housekeys to his face, testing the limits of modern plastic surgery. You comply.

8. Fee (Item to be remembered: bureau.) "Fee" always means a ticket to me. In this case, you might picture yourself driving a large bureau down the highway. Of course, you're pulled over and given a ticket for such an outrage, and you are told you must pay a fee of a thousand dollars immediately.

9. Pie (Item to be remembered: hair.) You wake up in the morning and walk into your bathroom; there, where your hairbrush should be, is a large lemon

merengue pie. You're so sleepy that you pick up the pie and start brushing your hair with it.

10. Toes (Item to be remembered: tile.) You are taking a shower, or trying to. The only problem is that water doesn't come out of the shower head—large ceramic tiles do. They fall to the ground and strike your toes. It's quite painful, and you can see your toes bleeding.

Here's where you can really start to impress yourself. I have reproduced the first ten keywords on the next page. If you have read and pictured the ten images I just gave you, now's the time to find out if you can remember the associations.

1 — (Tea. Remember that "t" and "1" each have one downstroke.)
What were you throwing iced tea into?

2 — (Noah. A "2" and an "n" are both written with a single curve.)
What did Noah have to do to attract animals?

3 — (May. A "3" and an "m" each have two distinct curves.)
What was the flower acting as?

4 — (Ray. Say "Four*rrr*.")
How did you make the sun feel better?

5 — (Leo. Latin L = 50.)
Who was the lion acting like?

6 — (Jaw. Handwritten "J" can mirror a "6.")
Who socked you in the jaw?

7 — (Key. First stroke of handwritten "K" can be a "7.")
What did you do with the key—and to whom?

8 — (Fee. Handwritten "f" has two strokes, like an "8.")
Why did you get that ticket?

9 — Pie. ("9" and "P" can be mirror images.)
What did you do with the pie?

10 — Toes. (See "1" above—and remember that the number with all curves is represented by the letter with all curves.)
What struck your toes?

How did you do? Well, I hope. If you feel comfortable with this list, turn the page for a pleasant surprise

Below is a list of the first ten Presidents of the United States. You just memorized it. You don't believe me? Take a look!

1. George Washington (WASHING machine)

2. John Adams (magazine AD)

3. Thomas Jefferson (CHAUFFEUR)

4. James Madison (MEDICINE)

5. James Monroe (Marilyn MONROE)

6. John Quincy Adams (QUEEN)

7. Andrew Jackson (Michael JACKSON)

8. Martin Van Buren (BUREAU)

9. William Henry Harrison (HAIR)

10. John Tyler (TILE)

How much grief could you have saved yourself in school if you had been able to master a list like that so quickly and completely?

The only possible snag in the above is the presence of the two Adamses, but by memorizing the Quincy part you've highlighted the difference between the two. Your instincts should tell you that there was no President Quincy, and help you put the name in the right place.

Here is my list of the first one hundred keywords.

1 Tea	34 Mayor	67 Check
2 Noah	(picture yours,	68 Chef
3 May	or City Hall)	69 Shop
4 Ray	35 Mall	70 Case
5 Leo	36 Match	71 Cat
6 Jaw	37 Mickey	72 Can
7 Key	(Mouse)	73 Gum
8 Fee	38 Mafia	74 Car
9 Pie	39 Map	75 Goalie
10 Toes	40 Rose	76 Cage
11 Dad	41 Heart	77 Cake
12 Tan	42 Rain	78 Cave
13 Team	43 Ram	79 Cap
14 Tire	44 Rear	80 Face
15 Tool	45 Rail	81 Foot
16 Dish	46 Rash	82 Fan
17 Tack	47 Rake	83 Foam
18 Dove	48 Roof	84 Fur
19 Tap (dancer)	49 Rope	85 Veil
20 Nose	50 Lace	86 Fudge
21 Note	51 Light	87 Fig
22 Nun	52 Lawn	88 Viva (picture
23 Enemy (Hitler,	53 Lamb	a cheering
for instance)	54 Lawyer	crowd)
24 Nero (picture	55 Lily	89 V.I.P.
a violin)	56 Latch	90 Boss
25 Nail	57 Lake	91 Bat
26 Nacho	58 Leaf	92 Bone
27 Neck	59 Lap	93 Bomb
28 Navy	60 Cheese	94 Bar
29 Nap	61 Jet	95 Ball
30 Mace	62 Chain	96 Bush
31 Mud	63 Jam	97 Back
32 Minnie	64 Chair	98 Puff
(Mouse)	65 Jewel	99 Pope
33 Mom	66 Judge	100 Thesis

I once knew a math whiz—the type who could do logarithmic tables in his head. When I explained to him how the "t-for-1" code enabled me to read numbers as words, and thereby memorize them easily, he seemed slow to understand. I went over it again. He shook his head. Surely, I thought, he must be able to grasp something so logical. Why was he so slow? "But," he said, "why do you need to encode these numbers? They're perfectly memorable to me. Numbers are my friends. They have family relationships and values that would be lost if I dressed them up as you suggest."

People with that kind of flair for numbers may not need to translate digits into sounds. But I can tell you that when it came time for me to study for my sergeant's examination, I was able to grasp all the definitions necessary, and could quote section numbers for hundreds of specific offenses—all thanks to the code we've studied in this chapter.

There are many like me who will never know the "language" of mathematics, and who are discouraged by the sight of numbers in an otherwise straightforward text. For us, the "t-for-1" code is a useful tool. That's why someone took the trouble to put it together, and that's why it has lasted so long.

A Party Trick

Here's a way to demonstrate how good a trained memory can be. It takes about fifteen minutes; your audience, whether a single person or a large gathering, will always be entertained and impressed.

Get your first twenty keywords down by heart by mastering strong mental images for them. Ask your audience to call out, one at a time, twenty objects for you to remember. Link each one to its corresponding number in the order they are memorized. Your helpers can pick simple and mundane items (table, pen, lightbulb) or complicated things (a mahogany bedside table with a damaged brass knob on the top drawer). It makes no difference.

Do not deliberately hurry the memory process, although you may find you need no more than fifteen seconds or so with an object. Some may be done almost instantly once you've had a little practice; in addition, some of the links may turn out to be easily memorable for you. Do not call for the next item until you have stored away the previous one. Resist the urge to backtrack and see if you can recall earlier words.

An independent witness must write down the numbers one to twenty, and, alongside each number, the objects in the proper order. This will be the checklist afterwards.

When you reach the final object, pause and ask if anyone else has tried to memorize the list along with you. One or two may say yes. Ask if they succeeded. They will admit they gave up after the first few items. You now recite aloud the list of objects from top to bottom. Occasionally, when performing this trick, you may find yourself stumped for one or two items. (This can only happen when your mental link is poorly chosen.) Don't worry about it. Come back to it later, or have the list-keeper prompt you. You won't forget it again.

Then, confident that you know the list (reciting it was the first chance you had to check), surprise your audience by reciting it backwards.

Now, really amaze them. Ask for numbers between one and twenty to be called out at random—then respond with the right object every time. Finally, you can ask to have objects called out and provide the corresponding numbers.

Believe me, this will have quite an impact on your friends! But you can do it after only a few hours of playing around with the "t-for-1" code.

CHAPTER NINE

Playing Cards

*"I am sorry I have not learned to play at
cards. It is very useful in life . . ."*
— Dr. Samuel Johnson (1709-1784)

The magician asks a volunteer to select a card at
random from a deck. He employs various tricks
and diversions, building anticipation. Halfway
through all the shenanigans, before the big finish,
he realizes to his dismay that, though the illusion
has gone flawlessly, he has forgotten what card he
is supposed to name!

Such stories are told even by professional
magicians. For my part, I'm not an accomplished
card player; "Go Fish" is about my speed. I do,
however, perform card tricks requiring me to locate and memorize cards. It helps to have a system,
and the "t-for-1" code is the best one I know of.
With it, you can commit to memory the sequence

of all or part of a deck of cards, and by keeping track of what cards have been put in play, you can, to a certain extent, harness the law of probability in games that are part chance and part skill. Some people may be able to do this instinctively; lucky them. I find the "t-for-1" code indispensable. My method has a codeword for each of the 52 cards.

As a conjuror, I perform several mystifying effects with cards, relying on a stacked (pre-arranged) deck, which I must first memorize completely. To do this I use a codeword for each playing card, and then mentally link each card's codeword with the keyword from the list we saw in the previous chapter. In this way, I can represent each card's position from one to fifty-two in the stacked deck.

Number (or Spot) Cards—Keywords

Non-face cards have keywords with the first letters telling you their suits. Clubs begin with the hard "k" sound; hearts begin with "h"; spades begin with "s"; diamonds begin with "d". The other consonant tells you the number or value of each card (see listing on facing page).

SPADES	DIAMONDS
2 – Sun	2 – Dane (picture Hamlet or a Great Dane dog)
3 – Sum	3 – Dame
4 – Sewer	4 – Deer
5 – Sail	5 – Doll
6 – Sash (picture a window)	6 – Dash (picture a footrace)
7 – Sack	7 – Deck
8 – Safe	8 – Diva (opera singer)
9 – Soap	9 – Dip
10 – Suits	10 – Dots

CLUBS	HEARTS
2 – Cane	2 – Hen
3 – Comb	3 – Ham
4 – Choir	4 – Hair
5 – Koala (bear)	5 – Hill
6 – Cash	6 – Hush
7 – Keg	7 – Hook
8 – Coffee	8 – Hive
9 – Guppy	9 – Hip
10 – Cats	10 – Hats

Aces and court cards, unlike the others, can suggest mental pictures. I don't use strict codewords for these. In the boxes that follow, you'll see how I picture them. You will want to replace these with your own images. Remember: my associations work for me because of my lifetime's worth of experiences. You may or may not see the logic in the connections. Don't try to absorb one of these unless it makes sense for you; be prepared to make up your own.

Aces

CLUBS: I picture a nightclub, like those I had to keep an eye on as a beat cop in the '50s.

HEARTS: As a boy I became fascinated with anatomy, and once actually bought a heart from the local butcher shop. So I think of that heart to remind me of the Ace of Hearts.

SPADES: There happens to have been a large hardware store in my home town that stocked all kinds of shovels (spades). I think of that establishment.

DIAMONDS: The idea of wealth is the key concept for me here.

Jacks

JACK OF CLUBS: Inside the nightclub, you'd find a gambler. I think gambling is stupid, and consider gamblers to be fools or, for our purposes, knaves. (A Knave, as you may know, is another word for the Jack of a suit.)

JACK OF HEARTS: Continuing with the idea of the Jack as a fool or "Knave," I ask myself: what kind of man is foolish in love? One answer: a man who is unfaithful to his wife. This is the operative idea for this card.

JACK OF SPADES: There was a rather slow teenager who always seemed to be minding the cash register whenever I had to make a purchase at the hardware store. I think of him.

JACK OF DIAMONDS: I picture a thief, in the stereotypical bowler-hat-black-eyemask-and-old-stogie mold.

Queens

QUEEN OF CLUBS: The wandering hostesses who kept tabs on the orders of nightclub patrons at the establishments on my beat form the image here.

QUEEN OF HEARTS: The ultimate female lover.

QUEEN OF SPADES: There is a scene in *The African Queen* in which Katharine Hepburn has the idea that saves the craft she and Humphrey Bogart must use to reach a German warship. She suggests welding a shovel-like attachment onto a broken propellor. Miss Hepburn, then, gives me the image for this card.

QUEEN OF DIAMONDS: On special occasions, Britain's Lady Di sports a glittering diamond tiara.

Kings

KING OF CLUBS: The club owner, of course.

KING OF HEARTS: My King of Hearts is a bridegroom.

KING OF SPADES: I think of a gardener for this card.

KING OF DIAMONDS: The person who handles the most precious stones for a living deserves the title King of Diamonds; I picture a jeweler.

Deck Sequence

Once you can quickly think of the image for each card, all that's left is to pair them mentally with the main keywords from one to 52. You can:

a) Memorize your own prearranged sequence (allowing you to "magically" name a selected card by sneaking a peek at the one above or below it); or

b) Simply use the images to keep track of which cards have been played in a given game. (But beware of those card games that use more than one deck!)

You might eventually get good enough to memorize cards as they are called off from a newly shuffled deck!

Sample Associations from My "Stacked Deck"
(Abbreviations: AD = Ace of Diamonds; 4S = Four of Spades; JS = Jack of Spades, and so on.)

11. (Dad)	KS (Gardener)	I picture my father out working in the garden, surrounded by huge plants he can't seem to get to behave
12. (Tan)	AH (Heart)	The heart I got from the butcher shop was tough, hard to dissect, almost like tanned leather.
25. (Nail)	7C (Keg)	A keg of beer skewered to the table by an enormous nail.
29. (Nap)	8S (Safe)	I notice that the door to a safe has been left open; a homeless person is sleeping inside.
38. (Mafia)	AD (Wealth)	Organized crime is full of "get-rich-quick" schemes that aren't worth pursuing.
42. (Rain)	7D (Deck)	The deck outside my house has been improperly sealed;

at the first sign of rain, it
rots away completely.

51. (Light) QD (Princess Di) The Princess is slim
                                ("light"); what's more, her
                                tiara sparkles.

That should give you the idea; there's really no point in giving you the whole list. After all, the associations are personal things, and an odd, ludicrous, or striking notion of your own is far better than one of mine. Your best bet is to work out your own. (Often, the simple act of writing the links down will be enough for them to register in your mind, though you should review them from time to time to be sure that they "stick.")

CHAPTER TEN

Exams

"Examinations are formidable even to the best prepared, for the greatest fool may ask more than the wisest man may answer."
— Charles Colton (1780–1832)

You've decided to study for a test. Have you resigned yourself to becoming a hermit—to long hours spent in solitary confinement, textbooks open, in total silence? Have you left strict orders with your friends, family, and loved ones not to be disturbed? If so, you're on the wrong track. That's probably the least effective method of study you can use.

You know full well, before you start, that you'll be bored stiff after five minutes of this. After ten minutes, with eyelids drooping, you'll find yourself reading and rereading the same paragraph over and over again, without absorbing it.

After fifteen minutes, you'll notice that the clock seems to have stopped, and you'll be looking for excuses to do so yourself.

Make It Easy

Acquiring knowledge can be fun for those who know how to go about it. It's a game that's never tiresome, a game you can return to again and again, where the hours pass by unnoticed, and you're so involved that only pointed remarks from others can drag you out of it. If you follow the advice in this chapter, you will find that study *can't* be tedious, and that you will dramatically increase your learning power. I know you may feel skeptical about this; hear me out!

First, abandon the silly idea that study has to be an unpleasant chore. Clever people are not any brighter than you or I; they don't work any harder to acquire their knowledge, either. They may actually spend less time studying—but they use that time well.

Time management means knowing the difference between being efficient and being effective. The world is full of efficient souls who do their absolute best at all they attempt; unfortunately, they are often not very successful. In fact, many are simply second-rate. Efficiency is "doing things right"; effectiveness is "doing the right things." Be selective. Confine your efforts to what will further your aims and objectives.

Clever people may even turn studying into a game. They definitely have better recall than others: they store facts and figures away where they can be easily retrieved. Well, you know how to do that now.

The "Aha!" Factor

Much so-called intelligence is just good memory. Creative individuals are quick to recognize patterns and connections: "Aha! I see; of course. Got it." When you say that, you are recalling a number of known facts and putting them into an order that suddenly sheds light on something you did not previously understand. That fresh concept can then be memorized and recollected when needed. It is an "Aha" experience. Aim to have more "Aha" experiences; they're good for your confidence and self-esteem. If you improve your memory, you'll feel brighter, too!

Use Your Five Senses

We all, when free from handicap, sample the world around us through use of our five senses: hearing, sight, touch, smell, and taste.

You learn better when you bring more than one of these senses into play. Mostly we rely on seeing while we read for ourselves, or on hearing when listening to people lecture. Even when the book is gripping, or the speaker has a flair for bringing a topic to life, this is an ineffective way to learn. That's why classrooms are equipped with blackboards, overhead projectors, or film screens: so you can be shown drawings and pictures, involving a second sense (sight) while being addressed. Still, most classroom work is limited to talk and chalk.

The best teachers, lecturers, tutors, and coaches will figure out some way to get students involved in a sensory way. By doing experiments in chemistry, carpentry, or cooking classes, for instance, the senses of touch, smell, and taste are engaged. Take a hint from these professionals: *always use as many senses as you can to memorize an important idea.*

Psychologists tell us smells make the most indelible memories. A smell can bring long-gone circumstances flooding back in detail after a lapse of years. What a pity that this sense often can't be used in private study or the classroom; students should try to poke their noses in more often.

A lecturer was stressing to his students how the pursuit of knowledge required them to be observant at all times. He produced a bowl of colored liquid and proceeded to demonstrate how to utilize all five senses. He held it up to the light and observed its color; he listened to how it splashed; he sniffed it; finally, he dipped a finger into it and conducted a taste test. Then he passed the container around the class for each student to do the same. As they tasted the liquid they screwed up their faces and exclaimed in disgust. It was foul. Afterwards, the lecturer said, "Now, ladies and gentlemen, that was a useful lesson in observation

120

with all your senses. I think it's one that will stay with you for a long time. By the way, how many of you noticed that the finger I dipped into the liquid was *not* the finger I put in my mouth?"

Choosing Books

What do you want to learn? Gardening? Cooking? A foreign language? How to pass a driving test? Chess? Public speaking? Pet care? Letter writing? How to sell your house? Weight loss techniques? Stand-up comedy?

Don't buy or borrow books just because they're included on someone's list of recommended reading. A helpful book for me might be useless to you. I once worked with a sociology graduate who boasted that he had never owned or read a book in his life. It wasn't strictly true, of course. He was making the point that students should dip selectively into textbooks, not try to read them cover to cover like novels. He was also hinting that most such books should be borrowed from public libraries (good advice, considering the price of books these days). The best candidate for actual purchase would be the book you borrow repeatedly because you find it indispensable.

Of course, in school or college, the required reading may have to come from set textbooks. In that case, you have no choice, but you should still try to supplement the main texts with other source material.

There is a way to determine if a book is right for you. First, find an abundant source of books on your chosen subject. Look in the front for the copyright date. If it's fifteen or twenty years old or older, you should probably put it back on the shelf. Life is changing so quickly the book may well be irrelevant. There are exceptions, of course, and you need to appreciate that texts on some subjects become out of date much less quickly than others. An old book on public speaking, for instance, may be a gem unsurpassed by anything else that's come out since, while an examination of computer programming methods may be hopelessly out of touch within a few months of release.

Next, look in the alphabetical index at the back of the book for any references to what you want to know. Look them up. Are they obviously readable? If the text demands diagrams or illustrations, are these provided, and are they clear? If so, you've found your book. If not, put it back and try another.

If you come across a book that's on the topic of your choice, but that really doesn't do much for you, *put it back!* Life is too short, and your time and energy are too valuable, for you to wrestle with complicated or obscure books. It's the author's job to engage *you*. If the print is too small, if there are algebraic formulas all over the place that you will never understand, if every page has imposing scholarly footnotes and cross-references, forget it. (Unless, of course, you're the academic type who appreciates all that. If that's the case, hold on to that book and get rid of this one.)

I have a trick I use to get past tough words or sentences while reading: I replace whatever I can't understand with the word "windmill." Often, further reading will clarify the obscure passage. Be warned, though: when too many "windmills" crop up on each page, that's the wrong book for you. Choose only books with very few "windmills."

I hope by now I've convinced you that studying should be easy. Stop trying to make it hard!

Using Books

Always read two or three books on the same subject. That way you will be told the same things in slightly different ways by the different authors. This will make the facts clearer and reinforce them. Information that shows up in all the books can safely be assumed to be fundamental and worth reviewing closely. Where writers differ, there is room for personal opinion.

I repeat: do not try to read textbooks. They are not stories but works of reference and study. Look up the part you need. Sort it out and file the data away in that mental filing cabinet of yours, where you can find it again later. Then shut the book. Soaking up knowledge a little bit at a time this way is fairly effortless; there's no need to become a recluse. Watch TV, play with the children, have friends and neighbors over, make conversation. Keep the book handy, however, because you might want to refer to it again before the day is over to find out the answer to some new question that pops into your head. And, yes, you can do that while carrying on a normal existence.

One advantage of owning textbooks is that you can write in them. I know we were taught as children not to "deface" books. That was then, when we lacked discretion—this is now. Most good students circle, underline, or highlight significant chunks of text. Being able to do this puts you at a distinct advantage, so deciding what books to buy should be part of your study strategy.

Notice how each paragraph in a book often has only one crucial sentence. All the rest is padding, enlarging on the original idea and giving examples. Underline that single sentence. Do it for the entire chapter; eventually you'll be comfortable doing it throughout the book. The sentences you highlight should, by themselves, form a continuous narrative and make sense. When you go back for review, *read only the underlined parts*. The complete book can be scanned in this way in only ten or fifteen minutes. You'll find, though, that the concentration you devoted to deciding which words should be underlined and which omitted will have given you a sound overall grasp of the material. This is because you employed the six guiding principles rather than simply trying to memorize the text.

Rote Learning—Right or Wrong?

Learning "by rote" means memorizing by means of repetition, with little or no attempt at understanding. Examples would include chanting multiplication tables, or reciting poetry or proverbs. The general approach is not looked on with favor by educational experts because lack of thought implies lack of comprehension. At its worst, rote learning could be brainwashing, with students conditioned into unquestioning acceptance of "facts" that are misleading or downright wrong, but that have become ingrained through repetition. Tests that rely too much on mere recall (facts, not thinking) are also condemned. Students, it is argued, can be overwhelmed by the amount to be absorbed, and may actually learn less as a result. Rote learning has become greatly discredited, and the feeling in some circles is that word-perfect learning is always wrong, or even indecent somehow; many tutors shy away from it.

I disagree with this view, and I cannot reject word-perfect learning altogether. Teachers are right to place greater emphasis on the so-called "higher" skills, such as the search for meaning and understanding, the critical faculties, the capacity for reasoned argument, creativity, logic, and problem-solving. That's fair enough. But we should not forget that these higher skills depend on a mass of memorized facts stored away for later recall. It is invaluable to be able to think "on your feet" in academic debate, sports, theatrical performance, industrial negotiations, a game of Monopoly, or a court of law. Those who do it best are those who can recall pertinent facts at will.

Through 25 years as a big-city cop, I had to meet all sorts of challenges, from facing down some bad guy who might attack me to resisting the court tactics of an astute defense lawyer. I couldn't carry around all the books I might possibly have needed: legal powers, duties, strong arguments, and much more all had to be kept in my head. Knowledge was all I had.

You can't run upstairs to check a book when you come face-to-face with a drunken ex-con who just made parole—and who went to jail because of your testimony; or when you detect a gas leak; or when you get a bomb threat over the phone. You have to have some set of fundamental procedures in place and ready for instant recall, even if they are only needed very infrequently.

This is not to say that *everything* should be memorized: far from it! I had no need to commit to memory the discipline and grievance procedures of my organization; they could be read and a course of action decided without the delay being harmful.

Homework

Put together answers to set homework questions with the aid of open textbooks and written notes. Take as long as you need. Spread the task over several days if you have to. Don't limit yourself by waiting until an exam looms to "turn on the gas." Concentrate on preparing a comprehensive and well-presented answer. Collect, collate, and edit all relevant data. The effort will teach you much more. And when you have to review materials, you will be reading first-class notes. By using the six guiding principles while working on homework, you'll remember a lot more.

Will you be able to perform at the same level under exam conditions? Yes. For a start, you'll know far more about each topic than you can possibly put down on paper. You'll have to be choosy about what you write. Contrast your enviable condition with that of the average student, struggling to dredge up enough decent material to pass. You won't have to pad; in ruthlessly eliminating material, you will offer a rich, distilled essence of all that you know. Under pressure and charged with excitement, you will write more—much more—than you could during a routine bit of classwork. Believe me, even on a bad day, you'll still be very, very good.

Shoot for the stars. Then, even if you go off course and miss, you'll end up very high.

Do the homework. It's essential. What you rehearse in your homework is what you will eventually produce at exam time. Remember that, despite the best efforts of examining bodies, tests have little or nothing to do with real life. This means that you shouldn't delude yourself: even if you are employed a certain way, or pursue a certain leisure interest, you may still have trouble with test questions if you don't study what's required of you. Absorb all the theory that you need, then use homework to practice airing that knowledge.

Create a style of writing and page layout that will be an automatic habit by the day of the exam.

Use only one pen (blue or black) for most of your writing, with another of a different color for headings, underlining, and so on. These two, along with a ruler, should probably also be employed for any sketches or drawings you include.

Memorize all diagrams you're likely to have to reproduce, so you can dash them off without thought as quickly as possible. Answers to some questions can be anticipated, prepared, and practiced beforehand. You should definitely commit to memory a few opening paragraphs that will help you get started on an answer or two. These are still more instances where rote learning (discussed earlier) can be justified. It beats sucking on your pen and staring at the ceiling for inspiration!

Must Knows, Should Knows, Could Knows

Mentally label everything you must learn. Each bit of information must fall into one of three categories.

> MUST KNOW
> SHOULD KNOW
> COULD KNOW

"Must Knows" are indispensable. You can't hope to pass unless you know them backwards and forwards. Then aim to pick up more steam by adding "Should Knows." "Could Knows" are little extras (quoting the source of a reference, say, or some details of the author). They can turn a good grade into an excellent one—but don't be distracted by them until you have satisfied the powers that be with enough from the first two categories. Focusing your mind on what goes into which category uses the six guiding principles and so aids effortless learning.

Demonstrate originality based on experience, if you can, but do not be unorthodox. (Your exam paper is definitely *not* the place to try out some idea not already known to the person who will mark it!)

If you can, take a look at past exam papers and specimen answers. Note the way previous questions are phrased and the frequency with which certain topics come up. While you can't expect to come up with a parallel list of questions to the ones you will actually face, you can, in the broad sense, learn what the examiners are looking for. The idea is to spot "Must Knows" and "Should Knows," extract them from study material, and file them securely in your long-term memory.

Epilogue

*"A memory is what is left behind when
something happens and does not completely
unhappen ... curry stains on the tablecloth
are an example."*

— Edward de Bono

Review of the Six Guiding Principles

1. MINUTES, not seconds

Learning anything takes a little time. A messy
room can be "tidied up" (or seem to be for the sake
of a laugh) by running a film backwards, so everything flies magically into place in a few seconds.
The process is, however, too quick and fleeting to
remember. You must allow time for new ideas to
sink in, and be prepared to go slower with the hard
stuff.

Most of us can think of a time when a problem
got the best of us. After a lot of stewing and sweat-
ing, we finally gave up. That night—or maybe

days later—the answer came to us "out of the blue." Or did it? What really happened was that your brain went on working out the problem, without you being aware of it, and only alerted you when it had something to report. What an ally!

Understand that you must do the work first. Absorb the data. Make an effort to sort it all out and understand it. Attempt to find solutions to problems. Once you've done all that conscientiously—and *not* before—it is a reliable technique to give up. Put the problem at the back of your mind; let your subconscious take a swing or two at the plate for you. If you've given it enough to go on, you'll eventually be surprised how clever it (you) can be.

2. EVALUATE

Take careful stock of your task. Don't just show up for the first lesson and trust that it will somehow make sense as the weeks go by. It won't.

Scan the entire syllabus. Break it up and rearrange it to suit you wherever you can. Bring forward topics you find simple: get them out of the way. Find out how much hard stuff there is. What will require a special effort later on? How much time will that take?

Adults in night school can often persuade instructors to vary course material to suit their needs, but it's not always possible to restructure the syllabus for other students. There is a way around this problem: persuade scholars and students who are further advanced than you are to show you their notes and handouts, or just discuss the material with them.

Read ahead. Find out what's planned for later; familiarize yourself with it now. You can understand and enjoy the subtle parts of a complicated spy thriller or murder mystery if you've seen the the film or read the book before. You know how it ends; you can concentrate more on how the clues connect within the plot. It's the same way with a course of instruction.

Your instructors may not be thrilled with your skipping around their rigid timetables. Of course, there must be an overall plan, but too strict an adherence to the calendar takes no account of the fact that you are human. You learn better in fits and starts. When you're enjoying yourself and making progress, don't let up. When the mood disappears (such as when you're sick or taking a long-overdue vacation), give it a rest with a clear conscience. You know from looking ahead and taking stock of the task when a renewed sense of urgency is required. Then you can return refreshed to study again.

3. MAKE AN EFFORT

Learning or remembering must be done by the learner. It isn't some sort of transmission process that emanates from the instructor. You don't absorb it through the pores by simply carrying around lots of the right books. Many students consider, at one time or another, dictating study material into a tape recorder so they can listen to it while driving the car or prior to going to sleep at night. A few claim it works. I doubt it works well.

It's just too passive. Learning is an active process. You have to involve yourself more than that. You remembered all the items in the rearranged dresser we discussed early on because you did it yourself. It wouldn't work if you merely watched someone else do it for you, or acted under someone else's directions.

The best trick I know for getting a grip on strange new material is to pretend I have to teach it to someone the next day. That way, I have no choice but to concentrate hard and ask myself: "What are the main points?" "How can I simplify it?" "Is there a code word that can make this memorable?" In determining the answers, I quickly master it myself.

4. ORDER THE DATA

Cleaning up that dresser, you had to put everything where it made sense, either in its own space or with something else. Memorize things the same way. Just about everything you learn can be linked to something else you already know. Sometimes, of course, you have to file a topic away in your head in a file labeled "new and strange," but that's pretty rare. The sooner you link another idea with it, the more certain you can be of retrieving both again.

Gaining knowledge is often an uncomfortable experience; try to have your peace of mind disturbed more often. "Whoa! Wait a second! Let's get this straight!" Upset your cozy notions with a new fact or two. Then restore calm to your troubled brain by sorting out the strange idea that has barged in. Once it makes sense, you learn. And a mind stretched by a new idea never returns to its old dimensions.

5. REINFORCE

Know-it-alls bore lesser mortals by displaying their knowledge; but they're not just showing off. My bet is that they are reassuring themselves that they can still recall a certain fact. By talking about what they know, they reinforce it. They like an audience to help them remember—but they'll usually take anyone who can be made to listen. Someone who knows enough to question, discuss, and occasionally correct them is better. So the best place of all for reinforcement is class. Try it yourself: quiz teachers, contribute to discussions. It really works. Newly acquired knowledge, especially, must not be left alone. Review it.

6. CURIOSITY

Tell me you don't like a subject, and I suspect at once that you don't understand it. If you don't understand it, how *can* you like it? Once you can understand it, it will intrigue you. Then you'll learn.

You'll learn most in the area that is a mystery to you. Welcome that sense of mystery, and accept that that is where there is most room for remarkable improvement. If you look at it this way, some of the dislike has to yield to cautious curiosity. Then you can muster the enthusiasm necessary to attack the subject.

Great self-confidence comes when you master a skill (theoretical or physical) that you had always assumed was beyond you. As a boy, I was unathletic—no, downright useless—when it came to ball games. In my forties, I trained to swim five to ten miles in cold open waters, and taught myself to Eskimo-roll in a kayak. At age 52 I could juggle and ride a unicycle. I walk tall with satisfaction at these achievements. I don't mean to boast. It doesn't matter to me that nobody I pass in the street is aware of what I can do. I know . . . and it makes me feel better. You can enjoy that feeling, too.